History
of the
Weimar Joint Sanatorium
and the
Weimar Cemetery

ROBIN YONASH

Cover photo: Weimar Institute Archives; photographer unknown

Published by the Colfax Area Historical Society
Colfax, California

Printed in the United States of America

ISBN: 1514332310
ISBN-13: 978-1514332313

DEDICATION

This book is dedicated to the courageous medical professionals and volunteers who continue to fight tuberculosis, which is second only to HIV as the leading infectious killer of adults worldwide.

CONTENTS

ACKNOWLEDGMENTS

Many thanks to Glenda Ragan for her assistance with researching the Weimar Cemetery.

1. History of the Weimar Joint Sanatorium

A. Legislative Background

In 1901 the California State Legislature passed the Indigent or Pauper Act which made county hospitals responsible for the care of the indigent sick, aged, blind, and physically disabled. At this time, county hospitals primarily served the dual purpose of hospitals for the indigent sick and almshouses for the aged and helpless poor.

Regardless of the legislation, counties took no adequate steps to meet the tuberculosis problem. Bills were repeatedly introduced to establish state TB hospitals. In the meantime, TB patients were housed in the same institutions as other sick and the aged.

In 1913 the state placed all institutions caring for tuberculosis patients under the State Board of Health. Inspections showed that county hospitals gave the homeless TB patients a place to die for no attempt was made at a cure. Statewide, the death rate from TB in 1915 was 189 per 100,000 population.[1]

That year the State began a $3.00 weekly subsidy [about $70/week in 2012 dollars] per patient if care met standards set by the State Bureau of Tuberculosis. Standards were established for construction and placement of buildings, care and treatment of patients, and diet.

For counties too small to maintain a special hospital for TB patients, the State assisted in setting up joint county institutions where the member counties participated on a pro-rata basis according to total property evaluation.

Between 1915 and 1931, counties spent a total of about $33,000,000 on

---

[1] TB was the scourge of its time. Compare this death rate to the 2004 rate of 121/100,000 for HIV/AIDS in the US. TB is still the second-most common cause of death from infectious disease worldwide (after those due to HIV/AIDS).

the construction and operation of tuberculosis hospitals with a state subsidy of $3,000,000. By 1931 the statewide death rate for TB dropped to 89 per 100,000—a decline of more than 50% over the 1915 rate.

B. Formation of the Weimar Joint Sanatorium

The Weimar Joint Sanatorium (WJS) was an effort on the part of 15 California counties[2] (see map on next page) to provide a place for the treatment of poorer tuberculosis patients who could not afford care in private institutions. One supervisor was chosen by each County Board of Supervisors to represent its county and the group thus formed was designated as the Hospital Central Committee of the WJS.

The WJS was located in Weimar, Placer County, California. Weimar is about halfway between Colfax and Auburn, just off of the Lincoln Highway (at the time), now Interstate 80.[3]

Climatic conditions were considered important at the time the Sanatorium was built, so a site was selected in Placer County in an area where the slogan was "above the fog and below the snow." Proximity to the Colfax School for the Tuberculosis, a private sanatorium under the direction of Dr. Robert A. Peers, was also a factor in the choice of the site. Dr. Peers was a medical advisor to the Hospital Central Committee in the establishment of the Weimar Joint Sanatorium and his expert knowledge of tuberculosis and his wide experience were invaluable to the committee.

A 408 acre site near Weimar was offered for the sanatorium by Charles Geisendorfer, Placer County Supervisor, and the foundation for the first building was laid in December 1918. This building was nearly completed March 14, 1919 when approximately 1,500 people, including members of the state legislature attended a celebration and barbecue at Weimar. This event was held to mark the establishment of a Northern California Tuberculosis Sanatorium.

The sanatorium opened on November 17, 1919 with 125 beds. In late 1922, the cost to care for a patient was $2.25 a day [about $40 in 2012 dollars]. The State Bureau of Tuberculosis contributed $3.00/day for each County patient; no subsidy was provided for paying patients.

---

[2] A group of supervisors from Placer, Contra Costa, Yolo, Colusa and Sacramento counties conceived the original idea. They were soon joined by six more counties: Amador, El Dorado, Plumas, Sutter, Tuolumne and Yuba. After the WJS opened, four more counties: Inyo, Nevada, Sierra and Solano joined, bringing the total to 15. In 1921 The San Francisco County Board of Supervisors voted to join, but this was vetoed by the Mayor.

[3] Legend has it that the Weimar derives its name from an old Maidu Indian Chief by the name of Weimuh. This was later corrupted to Weimar and is pronounced "Weemar" which distinguishes it from the German Weimar ["Wymar"].

Members of the Weimar Joint Sanatorium

Amador
Colusa
Contra
Costa
El Dorado
Inyo
Nevada
Placer
Plumas
Sacramento
Sierra
Solano
Sutter
Tuolumne
Yolo
Yuba

On June 19, 1921, a disastrous fire destroyed the kitchen, dining room, and small storerooms and damaged a Cottage and the Nurse's Home. The fire started in the kitchen and spread rapidly. Temporary buildings were quickly erected, and a decision to rebuild in concrete was soon made. The San Francisco architect H. H. Weeks was chosen to rebuild, using concrete, for $30,000.

Buildings were arranged on a unit plan with a central structure (administration and infirmary building) surrounded by dormitories and other structures and by pine and other trees, lawns and flowers. Half of the administration building was for men and half for women. At each end of the building was a glassed-in 12 bed ward. The central portion contained 24 private rooms, 12 for men and 12 for women. A heating system provided warmth in winter. The administration building also housed:

- Office of the Medical Director and assistants
- Receiving suite
- Examination rooms
- Sterilizing room
- Operating room
- X-ray room
- Laboratory
- Pharmacy
- Other offices
- Telephone exchange
- Chief Nurse's office
- Housekeeper's department
- Chart rooms
- Service rooms
- Diet kitchens
- Linen closets

The patient dormitories and cottages were unheated except for a wood stove in the dressing, bath, and locker rooms. Canvas covers kept rain and snow off the bedding. Stoneware hot water bottles (called "blind pigs") heated each bed during cold weather. During the summer the glassless windows allowed the dry mountain air to circulate as the only relief from the hot temperatures. As of December 1922, there were eight cottages for patients housed from twelve to eighteen men or women each and included:

- Day rooms
- Dressing rooms
- Locker rooms
- Bath rooms, shower rooms, lavatories and toilets

Service buildings and facilities included:

- Kitchen, ice plant, and cold storage building
  - The kitchen had steam cookers, food chopper, potato peeler, coffee grinder, and dishwasher – all operated by electricity
  - The dining room had two large steam tables to keep food hot during meal hours

- Four dining rooms; separate service and separate dishes were used for patients versus officers, nurses, and employees but all were served the same menu. Food service was cafeteria-style for those patients who were ambulatory. Meals were supplemented by snacks of milk and eggs (the WJS had its own herd of Holstein cows). Very ill or non-ambulatory patients were served on trays at their bedside. Special diets, including liquid, soft, and light meals, were provided as ordered by doctors.

- o Male ambulatory patients had the largest dining room as most patients were male
- o Female patients had a separate, smaller dining room
- o Officers and nurses dining room
- o Other employees dining room

- The Nurse's home provided accommodation for 30 nurses and included:

  - o Reception rooms
  - o Lecture and social hall
  - o Sun porch, which could be converted to a sleeping porch
  - o Dining room and kitchen
  - o Baths, lavatories, and showers
  - o Laundry room
  - o Trunk room

- Dormitories for male employees
- Power house
- Laundry
- Garage
- Office quarters for the Business Superintendent
- Two boilers, powered by crude oil, provided hot water, and steam for heating
- Incinerator
- Septic tank
- Pumping station for water from the Boardman Canal
- The Sanatorium also had a nursery, grade school, and high school to care for the children of mothers with tuberculosis (and presumably young patients with TB). There was also a library.

In August of 1938 a building was constructed by the W.P.A. on land deeded to the Indian Service, Department of Interior, for treatment of Indian tuberculosis patients. Eventually the Indians were moved to a large government sanatorium in Arizona. The building was later sold to the medical center for a token fee of $1.00.

Later the WJS entered into a contract with the Bureau of Indian Affairs to care for Indian tuberculosis patients of four western states. However, only Indians from Nevada and California were sent. They were placed with other TB patients.

According to an article in the Mountain Democrat, Placerville, California on January 17, 1946, the WJS property was valued at $1,006,484.48 [about $11.9 million in 2012 dollars]. Operating costs of the institution during the fiscal year ending July 1, 1945 were $2.72 per patient per day [$992.80 per year or approximately $11,700 per year in 2012 dollars]. The 15 counties had the following shares: Sacramento 31.82%; Contra Costa 22.99%; Solano 8.15%; Yolo 7.00%; Placer 4.97%; Colusa 4.64%; Sutter 4.37%; Yuba 3.55%; El Dorado 2.66%; Tuolumne 2.09%; Plumas 1.95%; Nevada 1.83%; Amador 1.76%; Inyo 1.56%; and Sierra 0.67%.

At its height in 1948, the sanatorium had 550 patients in twenty-four buildings. With over 300 employees it was the major employer for the people of Placer County, with a monthly payroll of $125,000 [about $1.2 million in 2012 dollars].

A school room, known as Sierra Hills School, was operated for children and youth who were patients at the center. In addition, adults were supported in studying for citizenship.

C. Life at the Weimar Joint Sanatorium

Entertainment, including movies, was provided, and patients could help in the gardens and with tending the grounds. There were two chaplains, Protestant and Catholic. Placards were posted to provide helpful hints and to dispel the belief that TB could not be cured. Occupational therapy was provided for ambulatory patients and bedridden patients were allowed to do needlework in bed. Patients were allowed to keep 50% of the proceeds from selling any handicrafts they made.

Still, patients frequently became depressed due to the severity of their infection and the hopelessness of a cure or because of separation from their families. In many cases it was difficult for family members to visit either due to the cost of travel or because of the fear of becoming infected themselves. Seeing other patients die was another source of despair.

Most of the WJS patients were men. The survival rate was about 50%. Some patients lived for several years at the WJS; some for only a few days. Many were discharged with the status "unimproved." Often patients left "against medical advice" and others ran away ("French leave"). Some committed suicide.

D. Treatment of Tuberculosis at the WJS

a. Eligibility

The WJS was open to all tuberculosis patients who were unable to pay for private treatment, who resided in one of the member counties, and who had lived in California for at least a year. Applicants had to obtain an admission card by applying to and being examined by their county physician. This card was then countersigned by a member of the Board of Supervisors from their county. Transportation was provided for those who could not pay the fare.

If a patient was able to pay, the charge [in late 1922] was $1.50/day [about $20.50 in 2012 dollars] and the WJS paid any balance above that.

b. Admission and Diagnosis

Upon arrival at the Sanatorium, a basic physical was done and then the patient was sent to bed for further observation. During this period a detailed physical was done, including a sputum test for TB and a X-ray. After a week or so, if the case was considered advanced the patient was assigned to a hospital bed, otherwise they went to a cottage.

Each patient had their temperature taken four times a day; was weighed weekly, and was visited at least once a day by the Medical Director. Patients rested daily from two to four p.m.

After a patient's temperature was normal for a week, they were allowed to go to the dining room for one meal a day; after a few more days they could go to two meals; and by the end of two weeks they could attend all meals. 30 minutes of exercise was allowed if the patient was not too weak.

c. Treatment

In the early 20th century, the only known treatment for tuberculosis was fresh air, sunshine, good food, and bed rest. At the time it opened, the WJS was considered a well-built, well-equipped institution.

As described by a booklet from the WJS, "the fresh air, sunshine, good food, and bed rest treatment was supplemented by the use of drugs and biochemicals for the alleviation of various distressing symptoms which may occur at times. Penicillin, streptomycin and other antibiotics were employed extensively and freely whenever the patients disease warranted their use. New procedures and new drugs were accepted as possible remedial agents as soon as sufficient experimentation had proved them safe and helpful.

"Certain surgical procedures also supplemented bed rest and offered the diseased tissues a quicker and safer "cure." Chief among those was the collapse of the affected lung by artificial pneumothorax. This was accomplished by introducing air into the space between the lung itself and the chest wall (the pleural space). By gradual instillation of increasing amounts of air the lesion was "squeezed" and walls of cavities, if present, were approximated. Thus the air in the pleural space "splints" the lung and allowed nature a chance to heal it. In some instances collapse of the lung was prevented by strands of tissue extending from the collapsed lung and adhering to the chest wall. If feasible, these were surgically removed. The procedure was known as "pneumonolysis."

"It was said, 'The home treatment of tuberculosis will be successful in direct proportion to the manner in which sanatorium principles are established and carried out. By the term 'sanatorium principles' is meant a carefully planned program of hygienic living, personal hygiene, regulated rest and exercise, food prescribed to suit the needs of the patient, and other measures which are directed toward increasing the patient's vitality and surrounding the patient with an atmosphere of cheer and hope.'"

E. After the Weimar Joint Sanatorium

Advances in medicine and methods of treatment eventually resulted in a reduced visit length per patient, as well as a substantial drop in the number of people afflicted with tuberculosis.

In 1957, the WJS changed focus to the Weimar Chest Center, treating other pulmonary diseases. In September 17, 1959 the board agreed to accept geriatric patients. The WJS was renamed the Weimar Medical Center in 1960 and in 1966 the Weimar Medical Center developed into a general community hospital and also started to take private patients.

By the time of the 50th anniversary in 1969 only 30 percent of the patients were TB cases. By then the monthly payroll at the center averaged over $150,000.

The hospital was closed in 1972 due to financial cuts by the state and counties. Following the closure, the property changed hands several times and in 1975 it reopened as Hope Village, a temporary relocation center for Vietnamese refugees. In May 1977, a group of Seventh-day Adventists purchased the property and it is now [2012] operated as the Weimar Center of Health and Education, AKA the Weimar Institute.

F. A Famous Patient

The most famous WJS patient was Pat Morita (who played Mr. Miyagi in the Karate Kid films). He was diagnosed with spinal tuberculosis at the age of two and spent the next nine years at the Weimar Joint Sanatorium in a body cast and unable to walk. Eventually he was transferred to the Shriner's Hospital in San Francisco where he received surgery to fuse four vertebrae in his spine. He was able to walk out of the hospital at age 11.

G. Sources for Weimar Joint Sanatorium History

(listed alphabetically):

Ben Nighthorse Campbell: An American Warrior by Herman J. Viola, Big Earth Publishing, 2002

"Booklet at the Weimar Institute" quoted in *Deaths and Burials at Weimar Sanatorium* by Patricia Stanford and Lois A. Dove, 1989 (The booklet itself is no longer in existence)

"Weimar Medical Center Celebrates Its 50th Anniversary", *Colfax Record*, November 16, 1969

Death and DALY estimates for 2004 by cause for WHO Member States

"[El Dorado] County Has $26,799 Share In Weimar Joint Sanatorium", *Mountain Democrat*, Placerville, CA, January 17, 1946

The Modern Hospital, Volume XIX, No. 6, December, 1922

Noriyuki Pat Morita: In the Footsteps of a Sensei by Charles C. Goodin

Weimar Center of Health and Education "About Us – History"

Weimar Joint Sanitarium by Melinda Herzog Landrith

Welfare Activities of Federal, State, and Local Governments in California, 1850-1934 by Frances Cahn, Helen Bary; Ayer Publishing, 1976

2. Weimar Joint Sanatorium Images

A Women's Building
Source: *Biennial Report*, State of CA Dept. of Public Health, 1921

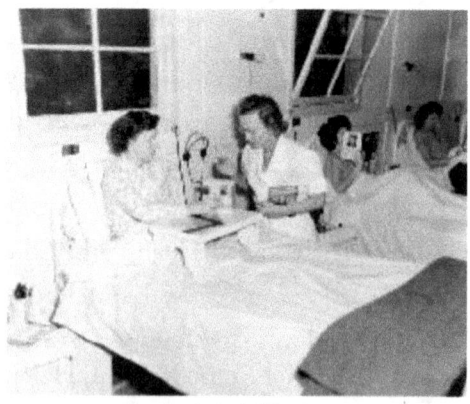

Patients in Ward
Source: Unknown

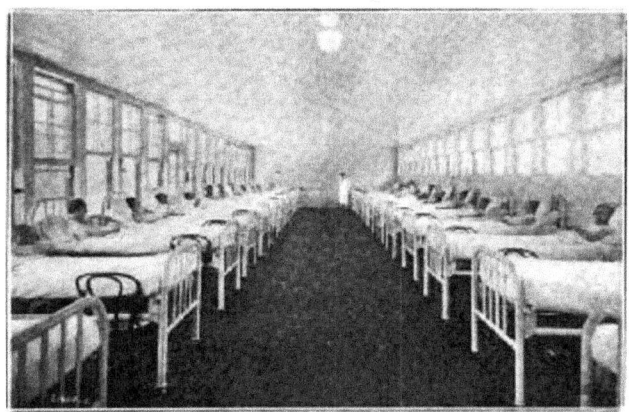

Sanatorium Ward
Source: *Biennial Report*, State of CA Dept. of Public Health, 1921

Source: *Images of Placer County* by Arthur Sommers, 2010

3. The Weimar Cemetery

A. History

The Weimar Cemetery was originally a part of the Weimar Joint Sanatorium (WJS) for tuberculosis patients, which operated under various names from 1919-1972. Patients who died at the Sanatorium and who had no other means of burial were interred on the Sanatorium property, AKA the Weimar Cemetery. Approximately 30% of the people who died at the WJS are buried in the cemetery.

Since this was essentially a "Potter's Field", instead of traditional tombstones each grave was assigned a number which was engraved onto a brass disc. The graves were marked by a piece of 2x6 wood with the corresponding brass disc attached. Sometimes the number was also painted on the wood.

Unfortunately, during various data transfers information was lost and errors crept into the remaining data, so until recently there was uncertainty about exactly who is buried in the Weimar Cemetery and where.

After the Weimar Joint Sanatorium, then called the Weimar Hospital, closed, the cemetery property was deeded to the Colfax Cemetery District. Over time, this fact was lost and only recently has it come to light. Further, when the property was transferred, no funds were included for maintenance.

After 1972, the cemetery was essentially ignored. The grave markers deteriorated and much of the cemetery grounds become clogged with brush so that many of the graves are no longer accessible.

A massive effort by volunteers, which included examining every Placer County death certificate for the 50+ years the cemetery was in operation, was undertaken in 2012. As a result, the names of the burials have been identified and in most cases the grave number is also known.

There are 1,474 persons buried in the Weimar Cemetery, not counting exhumations. See Chapter 4 for a list of names. All of the people in the list also have memorials on the Find a Grave web site (www.findagrave.com). Individual memorials may be found by going to the web site, clicking on the search link, entering the number from the FAG column of the list into the "Memorial #:" box, then pressing Enter.

Where the country of birth is known, just over half (51.1%) of the buried in the Weimar Cemetery were foreign-born and 48.9% were born in the United States. California was the top state, with 8.7% of the total and 17.8% of the US burials. Mexico accounted for 15.4% of the total burials and 30.1% of the foreign-born burials. Next was Italy, with 4.2% of total burials.

There are 34 known veterans of US military service buried in the Weimar Cemetery (33 are former patients of the WJS; one, Ernie Potterton, is a recent burial by the Weimar Institute). This number is primarily based on military data that was tracked on death certificates from March 1940 through 1967. There are certainly many other veterans in this cemetery, but it is not possible to identify all of them individually. **Veterans names are bolded** in the list in Chapter 4.

(Note that the Weimar Institute, the current owner of the former Sanatorium property, has added burials to the cemetery during recent years. These graves have traditional headstones, and are not considered part of The Weimar Project. The Weimar Cemetery itself is part of the Colfax Cemetery District.)

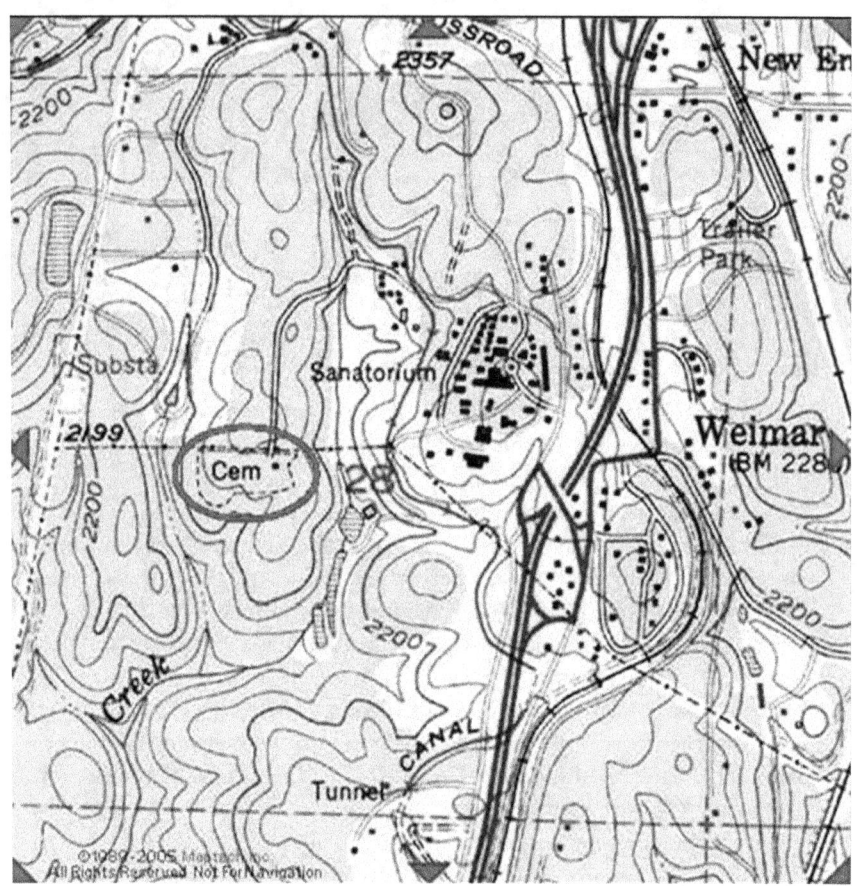

(Source of map: http://mapserver.mytopo.com)

B. Veterans in the Weimar Cemetery

Spanish-American War

Alexander, Henry

Kelly, James

World War 1

Adams, Douglas

Bell, Homer

Davidson, Raymond

Davis, Harry

Flores, Bennie D.
Army

Hallenborg, Roy V.
Army CAC

Kamensky, Alexander

Kelly, John Joseph

Massey, Raymond

Norton, George

O'Neil, Jack

Perry, Louis

Ramsdale, Chester

Sanwick, Clarence L.

Yee, Harry Bean

World War II

Baker, Lee
AKA Clark, Willie

Breedlove, Lee

Dougherty, Thomas
Army

Hendry, Frank
Army

Johnson, Phillip

Lewis, Henry

Norman, Lee
Air Force

Potterton, Ernest
Navy

St. Arnault, Robert E.
Navy

Other

Brighten, Jack
Army Infantry

Forkell, Edward

Gauthier, Peter

Holland, Charles
Army

Hovila, Archie

Maxwell, Joseph
Army

Nelson, Antone
Army

Spencer, William

C. Sources for Weimar Cemetery History

Death Certificates from the Placer County Clerk's Office
(note that exhumations and reburials were not always recorded on the death certificates)

Weimar Joint Sanatorium (WJS) records still extant:

Record	Date Range	Grave #
• Admissions Ledger #1	11/17/1919 – 12/31/1929	
• Admissions Ledger #2	01/01/1930 – 04/23/1919	
• Admissions Ledger #3	04/26/1939 – 11/16/1946	
• Admissions Ledger #4	missing	
• Admissions Ledger #5	07/01/1954 – 06/30/1959	
• Mortuary Record of Chief Nurse	04/20/1924 – 07/22/1934	176 – 612
• Mortuary Record of Chief Nurse	05/14/1944 – 08/31/1956	997 – A295
• Mortuary Record (Buried on Ground Cemetery)	09/01/1956 – 11/24/1972	A296 – A477
• Grave Book/Grave Numbers	04/09/1923 – 11/04/1972	108 – A477
• Grave Numbers Workbook	06/12/1937 – 11/04/1972	721 – A477
• Burial Cards (many are missing)	06/09/1939 – 11/04/1972	799 – A477

Deaths and Burials at Weimar Sanatorium by Patricia Stanford and Lois A. Dove, 1989 (based on the above WJS records)

Family Trees and other records on www.ancestry.com

Memorials on www.findagrave.com

4. Burials in the Weimar Cemetery

All of the people in the list below also have memorials on the Find a Grave web site (www.findagrave.com). Individual memorials may be viewed by going to the web site, clicking on the search link, entering the number from the FAG column below into the "Memorial #:" box, then pressing Enter.

The list is based on information that was available as of when the research was done in 2012. Additional or corrected information since then is recorded in the memorials on Find a Grave.

An "unk" in the Grave column indicates a burial located in the first 107 graves. The records for specific burials in these graves is no longer in existence. All we know is that they are buried in one of these graves.

Veteran names are **bolded**. Entries that are ~~grayed and crossed out~~ indicate people who were initially buried in Weimar and subsequently disinterred and reburied elsewhere. See the Find a Grave entry for details.

17

Robin Yonash

Name	Death Date	Birth Date	Birth Location	FAG	Grave
Abapo, Victoriano	13-Jul-1928	1899	Philippines	103714263	350
Aboitiz, Frank	8-Nov-1932	25-Oct-1877	Spain	103714264	533
Abyen, Paul	15-May-1936	22-Nov-1894	Slovenia	103714265	682
Aceves, Raymond	20-Oct-1969	1-Apr-1888	California	103052688	A467
Acosta, Frank	15-Feb-1949	28-Nov-1882	New Mexico	103714266	A175
Acosta, Margaret	19-Jul-1937	6-Oct-1922	California	103714267	725
Adams, Douglas	**9-Jan-1945**	**29-Nov-1885**	**Springfield, MA**	**97517857**	**A22**
Aguair, Manuel	29-Jan-1963	1892	unknown	103714268	A399
Aguilar, Ben	5-Jun-1927	1888	Mexico	103714269	290
Aguilar, Dionicia	29-Aug-1933	8-Apr-1899	Mexico	103714270	576
Aguilar, Jose	1-Feb-1938	1895	Mexico	103714271	753
Aguilar, Juana	17-Oct-1927	10-Feb-1918	Mexico	103714272	311
Aguilar, Regino	19-Nov-1924	1888	Mexico	103714273	178
Aguirre, Vidal	10-May-1947	28-Apr-1904	Mexico	103714274	A103
Aho, Jack	23-Jul-1947	5-Jun-1889	Finland	103714275	A112
Ahrens, Henry	6-Sep-1957	26-Sep-1883	Missouri	102318576	A315
Aiello, Salvadore—see Arello, Halvadore					
Alcorte, Joseph	19-Nov-1929	1892	Spain	103714276	404
Alexander, Henry	**22-Oct-1955**	**12-Jul-1884**	**Albany, NY**	**103714277**	**A271**
Alexander, James	13-Oct-1925	26-Sep-1855	New Mexico	103714278	233
Alick, Bart	18-Dec-1928	24-Aug-1877	Austria	103714279	369
Alik, Omar	16-Feb-1948	15-Jan-1907	Africa	103714281	A137

18

History of the Weimar Joint Sanatorium and the Weimar Cemetery

Name	Death Date	Birth Date	Birth Location	FAG	Grave
Allen, Charles J.	15-Jan-1956	17-Dec-1914	Ohio	103714283	A276
Allen, Elwood J.	24-Aug-1935	12-Jan-1894	California	103714284	661
Allex, Gust	27-Jul-1943	2-Feb-1894	Greece	103714286	958
Alm, Bert	17-Aug-1931	5-Nov-1880	Norway	103714287	490
Almirol, Rufino	8-Jan-1944	11-Jan-1908	Philippines	103714290	977
Alvarado, Antonio	25-Oct-1934	13-Mar-1907	Mexico	103714291	625
Alvarado, Frances	19-Dec-1921	4-Jun-1901	Mexico	103714292	unk
Alvarado, Jose	31-Oct-1944	1892	Mexico	103714293	A14
Alvarez, Joseph	26-May-1936	Feb 1902	Mexico	103714294	683
Amado, Manuel	21-Oct-1921	15-Mar-1896	Portugal	103714295	unk
Amavisca, Felipe	3-Mar-1925	2-Oct-1888	Mexico	103714296	199
Ammon, John M.	17-Mar-1939	20-Mar-1881	Humboldt Co., CA	103714297	792
Anderson, Andy	1-Jun-1941	3-Dec-1880	Finland	103714298	873
Anderson, John Andrews	24-Jul-1954	22-Jun-1875	Michigan	103714299	A256
Anderson, Lee	9-Jan-1928	17-Jun-1874	Indiana	103714301	324
Anderson, Niels	7-Jun-1939	13-May-1885	Denmark	103714302	799
Anderson, Victor	23-Oct-1961	13-Oct-1894	Denmark	103714303	A383
Andreotti, George	23-Sep-1941	22-Apr-1881	Italy	103714304	885
Andreque, Gregoria	12-Mar-1932	1892	Mexico	103714305	515
Angelos, Christ	18-Jun-1924	Jul-1891	Greece	103714306	160
Angle, John	21-Jun-1962	9-Dec-1888	Finland	103714307	A394
Angove, James	15-Dec-1932	12-Apr-1865	England	103714308	544

19

Robin Yonash

Name	Death Date	Birth Date	Birth Location	FAG	Grave
Anriqueta, Cabrera	31-May-1925	1900	Mexico	103714309	211
Antell, Hjalmar Erickson	4-Aug-1947	27-Jun-1903	Finland	103714310	A115
Antures, Alfredo	15-Sep-1929	18-Jun-1904	Mexico	103714311	400
Arellano, Arcadio Cruz	8-Mar-1946	12-Jan-1890	Mexico	103714312	A60
Arello, Halvadore	24-Jan-1920	11-May-1880	Sicily	99561339	unk
Argeris, George	5-May-1924	14-Feb-1885	Greece	103714313	153
Arias, Arthur	11-Aug-1935	28-May-1907	Mexico	103714314	660
Arroyo, Fidencia	8-Jul-1928	15-Nov-1914	Mexico	103714315	347
Arroyo, Lue Santos	27-Apr-1928	15-May-1882	Mexico	103714316	340
Arroyo, Octavio	4-Jul-1947	22-Mar-1906	Mexico	103714317	A110
Arthur, William Thomas	21-Feb-1939	16-Jun-1892	Hiattville, KS	103714318	790
Ascension, Victoria	25-May-1963	11-Dec-1872	Mexico	103714319	A406
Atwood, Margaret	24-Dec-1930	25-Aug-1887	Montana	103714320	451
Aurell, Edward	27-Mar-1944	10-Feb-1893	Finland	103714321	990
Austin, Richard	3-Sep-1934	14-Nov-1913	Kentucky	103714322	617
Avila, Lazaro	13-Sep-1924	1903	Mexico	103714323	167
Aviso, Vincente	20-Feb-1930	14-Aug-1902	Philippines	103714324	412
Ayala, Leandro	16-Jun-1943	17-Jun-1901	Mexico	103714325	951
Bachmor, William	10-Oct-1955	1-Jan-1872	Germany	103714326	A269
Bader, Howard	6-Dec-1960	20-Sep-1907	Hooper, NE	103714327	A367
Baker, John	28-Apr-1923	8-Dec-1884	Poland	103714328	113
Baker, Lee	**21-Jan-1959**	**23-Dec-1913**	**Illinois**	**97532543**	**A340**

20

History of the Weimar Joint Sanatorium and the Weimar Cemetery

Name	Death Date	Birth Date	Birth Location	FAG	Grave
Ballard, Robert Earl	11-Nov-1950	21-Jan-1893	Chicago, IL	103050801	A211
Ballum, Lewis	27-Mar-1944	5-Jan-1907	Joliet, IL	103714329	991
Baltierra, Eleuterio	30-Aug-1968	4-May-1900	Mexico	103714330	A463
Bangle, Ben	28-Dec-1921		California	103714331	unk
Banks, Fay Lee	13-Nov-1940	13-Jul-1913	Pine Bluff, AR	103714332	855
Barate, Ernesto	9-May-1931	1883	California	103714333	474
Barer, John J.	6-Jan-1935	27-Sep-1883	Russia	103714334	634
Barett, Charles	11-Aug-1929	23-Mar-1864	New York	103714335	393
Barni, Andy	28-Mar-1949	19-May-1876	Italy	103714336	A178
Barrera, Amando	19-Jul-1925	24-Feb-1893	Mexico	103714337	220
Barrozo, Marie	23-Aug-1921		Portugal	103714338	unk
Barry, Henry	9-Mar-1923	12-Feb-1867	Pennsylvania	103714339	unk
Barry, John	23-Aug-1930	11-Oct-1872	New York	103714340	433
Bartlett, John B.	3-Jan-1928	15-Jan-1865	New York	103714341	321
Batara, Agapito	20-Mar-1939	15-Mar-1910	Philippines	103714342	793
Bateman, Luther	22-Dec-1927	18-Dec-1891	Oklahoma	103714343	320
Battero, Toni	29-Nov-1927	29-Aug-1890	Italy	103714344	318
Baubel, Max	27-Jan-1957	6-Feb-1900	Germany	103714345	A301
Bauers, Fred	10-Nov-1932	20-Oct-1886	Germany	103714346	534
Baum, James	13-Jan-1923	31-Dec-1862	Indiana	101805097	unk
Bayes, Charmie	18-Feb-1935	20-Jan-1914	Virginia	99272633	640
Bazileff, Mike	3-Jul-1941	18-Dec-1905	Vladivostok	103714347	878

21

Robin Yonash

Name	Death Date	Birth Date	Birth Location	FAG	Grave
Beams, John Dirk Crowder	26-Dec-1958	22-Nov-1885	Oklahoma	103714348	A339
Becerra, Socorro	21-Dec-1937		Mexico	103714349	742
Beck, John	6-Mar-1943	10-Aug-1882	Finland	103714350	935
Beldean, Edward	6-Dec-1924	15-Apr-1885	Italy	103714351	182
Belding, Wallace	16-Mar-1943	10-Apr-1904	Ogden, Utah	72896711	936
Bell, Earl	23-Sep-1936	27-Mar-1892	Missouri	103714352	691
Bell, Homer	**17-Jun-1962**	**6-Apr-1893**	**Indiana**	**97583316**	**A393**
Bender, John	5-Apr-1931	15-Dec-1891	Austria	103714353	469
Bendixon, Nels	22-Mar-1944	2-Dec-1885	Denmark	103714354	989
Benton, Baby No. 1 and No. 2	15-Apr-1943	15-Apr-1943	Weimar, CA	103714355	941
Benton, Charles S.	9-Dec-1941	20-Aug-1900	Lemoore, CA	103714356	889
Bergen, Harry F.	13-Nov-1939	10-Oct-1884	New Orleans, LA	103714357	815
Berkley, Joseph Newman	28-Oct-1940	13-Sep-1878	Central City, SD	103714358	850
Berttochetti, Bert	19-Jun-1961	19-Mar-1887	Austria	103714359	A377
Bidwell, William	10-Oct-1928	10-Apr-1866	England	103714360	363
Bietz, John	7-Jun-1925	9-Feb-1873	Romania	103714361	212
Bijcdick, Zulfo	16-Jun-1931	25-May-1887	Austria	103714362	482
Bilich, Antone	17-Sep-1925	5-May-1867	Slavia	103714363	230
Birdsall, Arthur E.	29-Oct-1927	28-Oct-1880	Colorado	103714364	313
Blamire, Edward	25-Jul-1953	11-Oct-1891	England	103714365	A241
Blanco, Jose	7-Sep-1935	14-Sep-1901	Mexico	103714366	663
Blankenship, Henry	10-Jun-1966	15-Oct-1880	California	102198755	A435

22

Name	Death Date	Birth Date	Birth Location	FAG	Grave
Boca, Telesforo	13-Aug-1930	5-Jan-1902	Mexico	103714368	429
Bock, Otto	9-Jun-1926	9-Jun-1889	Germany	103714370	257
Bodi, George	12-Dec-1935	24-Apr-1877	Hungary	103714371	673
Bogun, Fred	25-Oct-1925	20-Jul-1878	Michigan	103714372	236
Bolanos, Lupe	11-Nov-1939	12-Dec-1909	Mexico	103714373	814
Bonner, Clifford	10-Dec-1944	29-Oct-1905	Wisconsin	102251946	A17
Borella, Harold	16-Dec-1948	17-Sep-1880	Denmark	103714374	A171
Botello, Angelo	11-Jul-1929	16-Aug-1893	Mexico	103714375	388
Boyanges, Theodore	28-May-1924	25-Mar-1872	Greece	103714376	157
Bradsbury, George F.	9-Nov-1921	25-Jan-1899	Washington	103714377	unk
Bradshaw, Charles	15-Jan-1925	17-Jul-1851	Canada	103714378	190
Brady, Jack	8-Jul-1935	1-Feb-1867	California	103714379	656
Brady, William	21-Aug-1933	16-Jun-1907	New York	103714380	575
Bragga, Joseph L.	9-Oct-1931	23-Sep-1895	Azores	103714381	498
Brakebill, Ralph	19-Jul-1959	27-Jan-1909	Arkansas	102322017	A344
Brant, Carl	9-Dec-1936	2-Feb-1888	Cleveland, Ohio	103714382	705
Bratton, Richard	27-Aug-1936	23-Jan-1871	Kansas	103714383	688
Bravo, Frank	17-Mar-1963	24-Aug-1865	Mexico	103714384	A404
Breedlove, Lee	**13-Sep-1972**	**5-Dec-1919**	**Arkansas**	**103714385**	**A476**
Brent, John Oliver	26-Feb-1957	16-Jan-1885	New York	103714386	A302
Brett, James	2-Mar-1929	21-Jun-1880	Ireland	103714388	376
Brewis, Harry	17-Apr-1964	21-Jun-1886	California	103714389	A416

23

Robin Yonash

Name	Death Date	Birth Date	Birth Location	FAG	Grave
Bridgewater, Harry	4-Mar-1938	21-Jul-1889	Barry, IL	103714390	758
Brigham, Howard	2-May-1945	23-Mar-1923	Nevada	103714392	A32
Brighten, Jack	**13-Jul-1960**	**5-Jun-1905**	**Holbrook, AZ**	**97453540**	**A361**
Brooks, Ples	20-Nov-1948	31-Dec-1875	Texas	103714393	A168
Brown, Daniel Souza	21-May-1946	2-Nov-1893	Hawaii	103714394	A71
Brown, Ernest L.	16-May-1931	22-Jan-1880	Nevada	103040915	476
Brown, George	16-Jan-1921	13-Jun-1872	Canada	103714395	unk
Brown, John	13-Nov-1929	26-Feb-1874	New York	103714396	403
Brown, John	10-May-1945	9-Jun-1924	Gallup, NM	99285503	A33
Brown, Samuel	6-Aug-1947	17-Nov-1899	California	103714397	A116
Brown, Stella	8-Feb-1931	29-Jul-1902	Minnesota	103714398	457
Brown, Walter—see Prijatel, Charles (birth name)					
Brown, William	13-Dec-1942	2-Jan-1885	Ireland	103714399	924
Bucci, Natali	14-Aug-1930	25-Dec-1882	Italy	103714400	430
Buckna, George Arthur	30-Jun-1945	5-Aug-1900	East Helena, MT	103714401	A40
Buhlilsky, William	29-Oct-1939	9-Jan-1866	Russia	103714402	812
Burke, Edward Joseph	13-Apr-1923	15-Sep-1872	West Virginia	103714403	109
Burkett, Audie	3-Nov-1972	7-Mar-1891	Missouri	103604467	A477
Burnett, George	15-Jul-1939	15-May-1900	Needles, CA	103714404	804
Burnett, Sharlene	26-May-1939	12-Oct-1938	Sacramento, CA	103714405	798
Burns, James	27-Oct-1925	11-Feb-1890	Pennsylvania	103714406	237
Burns, John	8-Jul-1941	15-May-1886	Minneapolis, MN	103714407	879

24

History of the Weimar Joint Sanatorium and the Weimar Cemetery

Name	Birth Date	Death Date	Birth Location	FAG	Grave
Bustos, Fausto	3-Oct-1907	9-Feb-1935	Mexico	103714408	638
Butler, William A.	27-Mar-1871	24-Apr-1924	Minnesota	103714409	151
Butulio, Nick	15-Aug-1891	18-Nov-1935	Yugoslavia	103714410	669
Byrd, Garlen	1-Jan-1884	30-Dec-1937	Missouri	103714411	745
Byrd, Herbert	6-Mar-1899	23-Nov-1947	Mississippi	103714412	A131
Caballero, Aurelio	14-Nov-1885	28-Mar-1957	Mexico	103714413	A308
Cabor, Mike	25-May-1885	15-Jan-1930	Yugoslavia	103714414	410
Cabral, Epifanio Espinosa	7-Apr-1909	14-Jul-1931	Mexico	103714415	486
Cabrera, Felipe	26-May-1881	16-Aug-1953	Mexico	103714416	A242
Cabrera, Gabriel Bargas	24-Mar-1898	3-Feb-1944	Mexico	103714417	982
Cadena, Felix	Nov-1895	27-Jul-1932	Mexico	103714418	524
Caldeo, Eugene	15-Nov-1899	7-Nov-1923	Philippines	103714419	131
Camarena, Tiburcio	11-Aug-1902	9-Dec-1951	Mexico	103714420	A226
Cameron, Daniel	12-Nov-1871	10-Oct-1960	Canada	103714421	A363
Camicia, Nick	12-Jan-1886	1-Feb-1941	Italy	103714422	865
Campbell, Arthur	12-Nov-1872	30-Nov-1933	Iowa	103714423	588
Campbell, Colin	10-Oct-1864	1-Oct-1930	Canada	103714424	442
Campbell, William	11-Nov-1880	22-Mar-1933	California	103714425	555
Campillo, Ramon	28-May-1899	4-Feb-1944	Mexico	103714426	983
Campos, Raphael	24-Oct-1900	14-Oct-1924	Mexico	103714427	169
Capps, Austin	30-Dec-1905	14-Aug-1967	Colorado	103714428	A453
Capps, Lillian	30-Apr-1912	2-Jul-1937	Canada	103714429	723

25

Robin Yonash

Name	Death Date	Birth Date	Birth Location	FAG	Grave
Captell, William	1-Aug-1935	4-Jul-1875	Wisconsin	103714430	657
Caretto, Jim	12-Feb-1933	15-Oct-1886	Italy	103714431	551
Carlin, Patrick	7-Dec-1923	17-Mar-1843	Ireland	103714432	133
Carlson, August	2-Aug-1937	3-Jun-1869	Sweden	103714433	730
Carlson, George	16-Dec-1958	7-Jul-1890	Sweden	103714434	A338
Carmichael, Raymond	26-Dec-1928	8-Jan-1900	New York	103714435	370
Carpenter, John G.	26-Sep-1943	24-Jun-1891	Granville, NY	102251195	966
Carraher, William J.	20-Sep-1938	9-Mar-1864	Wheatland, Iowa	102229691	774
Carrera, Rafael Navarez	24-Apr-1952	24-Oct-1901	Mexico	60064935	A230
Carroll, Benjamin	20-May-1929	15-Jan-1867	Ireland	99269833	384
Carroll, Michael J.	3-Jan-1950	8-Sep-1890	Ireland	103714436	A197
Carter, Aaron	8-Dec-1949	7-Jun-1917	Florida	103714437	A194
Carter, John	8-Sep-1931	22-Jun-1879	North Carolina	103714438	494
Cartwell, Fairlee	29-Oct-1925	5-Nov-1885	Nebraska	103714439	238
Casarez, Antonio	27-Apr-1925	1903	Mexico	103714440	207
Casci, Ruth	19-Dec-1949	18-Dec-1898	Ohio	103714441	A195
Casciani, Tobia	13-Oct-1922	20-Oct-1862	Italy	103714442	unk
Castanada, Lorenzo	4-May-1932	1888	Mexico	103714443	520
Casteel, Bert	9-Jun-1925	24-Jun-1876	Illinois	103714444	213
Castini, Gemas	1-May-1933	22-Oct-1885	Italy	103714445	558
Cathman, Harold	27-Dec-1931	10-Jun-1917	California	103714446	508
Cavanaugh, George	4-Aug-1934	26-Oct-1872	Pennsylvania	103714447	614

History of the Weimar Joint Sanatorium and the Weimar Cemetery

Name	Death Date	Birth Date	Birth Location	FAG	Grave
Cavazzi, Joseph	3-Sep-1944	15-Jun-1879	Italy	103714448	A9
Cavizo, Mina Rolene	16-Mar-1946	16-Mar-1923	California	103714449	A61
Cechet, Frank	28-Nov-1931	20-Dec-1887	Italy	103714450	503
Ceja, Cecilia	25-Jan-1932	1898	Mexico	103714451	513
Cerero, Stanley	30-Dec-1931	5-May-1883	Philippines	103714452	509
Cervantes, Francisco	1-Mar-1946	1-Jun-1909	Mexico	103714453	A59
Cervantes, Jose	25-Oct-1945	19-Mar-1897	Mexico	103714454	A52
Cervini, John	12-Apr-1943	16-Jan-1878	Italy	103714455	940
Chaigres, Jesus	29-Mar-1957	3-Jul-1910	Mexico	103714456	A309
Champlin, William	23-Jul-1949	1-Dec-1898	New York	103714457	A186
Chan, John Bun	4-Sep-1958	17-Apr-1891	China	103714458	A333
Chan, Stanley	30-Mar-1945	9-May-1893	China	103714459	A30
Charles, Tony	17-Jul-1920	3-Jan-1884	Mexico	103714460	unk
Chavaria, Antonio	11-Dec-1942	12-Mar-1884	Spain	103714461	922
Chavarria, Antonio	22-Jan-1944	4-Dec-1885	Mexico	103714462	980
Chavez, Grabiel	21-Dec-1944	Mar-1871	Mexico	103714463	A19
Chavez, Nicholas	9-Dec-1934	10-Sep-1865	Arizona	103714464	630
Chavez, Pedro	12-Jan-1942	27-Jan-1897	Mexico	103714465	892
Check, Hom—see Hom, Check					
Chessman, Perry	22-May-1954	20-Feb-1887	Nebraska	102318323	A254
Chiari, Frank	27-Mar-1931	31-Aug-1879	Italy	103714466	463
Chong, Chin	24-Jan-1934	14-Apr-1894	China	103714467	593

27

Robin Yonash

Name	Death Date	Birth Date	Birth Location	FAG	Grave
Chovet, Andrew	13-Mar-1929	16-Apr-1910	California	103714468	379
Christensen, Harold	15-Jan-1927	3-Jul-1899	Denmark	103714469	280
Christian, Marks	14-Jun-1926	15-Jan-1862	Sweden	103714470	258
Christie, Oscar	2-Jan-1944	30-Mar-1884	Norway	103714471	976
Cinbal, Francisco	12-Aug-1929	4-Oct-1908	Philippines	103714472	394
Clark, Andrew	29-Nov-1935	14-Mar-1882	Michigan	103714473	672
Clark, Charles	24-Nov-1931	23-Nov-1885	Pennsylvania	103714474	502
Clark, John	19-Jun-1938	21-Nov-1885	England	103714475	770
Clark, Walter J.	22-Oct-1949	18-Nov-1884	New York	103714476	A191
Clark, Willie—see Baker, Lee (death certificate has both names)					
Clarke, Robert E.	8-Jul-1943	12-Oct-1892	Shreveport, LA	103714477	954
Clausen, Martin	20-Oct-1943	16-Jun-1901	Chicago, IL	103714478	970
Clayton, Frank	27-Dec-1943	4-Mar-1876	Dayton, Ohio	103714479	974
Clements, Elbert E.	10-Oct-1959	4-Nov-1906	Texas	101799895	A347
Cobo, Alfredo	21-Oct-1926	1-May-1885	Spain	103714480	273
Cochran, Charles	28-Feb-1957	7-Sep-1902	New Mexico	103714481	A304
Coco, Joe	7-Feb-1925	28-Jan-1882	Italy	103714482	194
Coitot, Joe	26-Jul-1920	6-Apr-1863	Italy	103714483	unk
Coleman, Herman	24-Sep-1934	3-Jul-1886	Finland	103714484	620
Collias, Anthony	15-Jul-1939	1883	Greece	103714485	805
Collins, Arthur	10-Sep-1946	24-Jul-1904	West Virginia	103714486	A75
Collins, Charles	8-Dec-1929	27-Oct-1890	Ireland	103714487	406

History of the Weimar Joint Sanatorium and the Weimar Cemetery

Name	Death Date	Birth Date	Birth Location	FAG	Grave
Collins, Tom	15-May-1926	2-Apr-1869	New Hampshire	103714488	253
Colran, Henry	25-Aug-1955	19-Oct-1883	Dawson Co., GA	103714489	A267
Columbus, Romero	11-Nov-1934	19-Dec-1901	Portugal	103714490	627
Cominolo, Louis	9-Jun-1930	18-Nov-1882	Italy	103714492	421
Connell, Frank	28-Oct-1945	28-Oct-1888	Philadelphia, PA	103714493	A49
Connelly, Charles	27-Feb-1923	21-May-1860	Ireland	103714494	unk
Connors, Patrick	22-Jan-1948	6-Jun-1887	Ireland	103714495	A135
Conrad, George E.	1-Mar-1956	29-Dec-1897	Wisconsin	103714496	A281
Conroy, Phil	20-Mar-1931	14-Jan-1885	Ireland	103714497	461
Contreras, Ciriaco	12-Aug-1925	18-Jun-1908	Mexico	103714498	226
Cope, Henry	16-Jul-1933	14-Oct-1892	Arkansas	103714499	569
Copeland, Shafer	17-Apr-1954	8-Jul-1892	Stockton, CA	103714500	A252
Coronado, Cuspir	1-Apr-1928	24-Oct-1885	Mexico	103714501	335
Corpus, Liberato	30-Aug-1930	29-Dec-1895	Philippines	103714503	437
Corral, Epigmenio	3-Aug-1937	Mar-1904	Mexico	103714504	731
Corson, William	28-Jun-1941		unknown	103714505	877
Cortez, Jose Aguilar	21-Mar-1954	19-Apr-1888	Mexico	103714506	A251
Cost, Pete	4-Aug-1925	5-Feb-1896	Greece	103714507	222
Costa, Mary Helen	20-Apr-1924	22-Mar-1906	Rhode Island	103714508	149
Costa, Raffaelo	4-Jun-1944	18-Apr-1875	Italy	103714509	A2
Cota, Juan	24-Sep-1938	24-Jan-1896	Mexico	103714510	775
Craig, Fred	31-Jul-1934	2-Sep-1875	Canada	103714511	613

29

Name	Death Date	Birth Date	Birth Location	FAG	Grave
Craig, James	12-Sep-1953	27-Aug-1898	Wisconsin	103714512	A244
Cramton, Hollis	28-Apr-1958	17-Dec-1905	Hadley, MI	102196110	A326
Crawford, Harry E.	15-Dec-1930	15-Mar-1868	Ohio	103714513	449
Crawford, James	31-Dec-1932	2-Dec-1890	Missouri	103714514	545
Crawford, Robert	23-Oct-1955	10-May-1900	North Carolina	103714515	A270
Criste, Marcelino	5-May-1940	16-May-1913	Philippines	103714516	831
Crosby, George	11-Jul-1943	14-Aug-1908	Zanesville, Ohio	103047896	955
Cross, Henry	6-Dec-1940	5-Mar-1897	Shawnee, OK	99519672	858
Cross, Myrtle Maud	2-Jun-1928	2-Jan-1881	Iowa	103714517	343
Cuaresma, Marion	2-Oct-1948	4-Jul-1876	Philippines	103714518	A162
Cubada, John	20-Aug-1932	5-Aug-1855	Italy	103714519	527
Cummings, Ernest	23-Dec-1964	18-May-1903	Massachusetts	103714520	A422
Curche, Bruno	20-Apr-1928	15-Dec-1882	Italy	103714521	338
Curry, Edward O.	16-Jan-1920	10-Aug-1885	Michigan	103714522	unk
Curry, Moses	4-Apr-1951	2-Jun-1921	Oklahoma	103714523	A218
Curtin, Dave	25-Apr-1924	16-Jan-1865	Ireland	103714524	152
Curtis, John	5-Nov-1923	3-May-1860	New York	103714525	130
Daglio, Ethore	16-Mar-1924	28-Mar-1892	Italy	103714526	144
Dahl, Olaf	30-Jan-1947	21-Mar-1883	Norway	103714527	A90
Daich, Nicholas	8-Aug-1925	23-Oct-1886	Serbia	103714529	225
Daisch, Eso	19-Aug-1928	1877	Siberia	103714530	354
Dale, James	13-Sep-1931	26-Jan-1888	New York	103714531	495

30

Name	Death Date	Birth Date	Birth Location	FAG	Grave
Daley, Harry	16-Jan-1929	10-Nov-1888	Montana	103714532	374
Daley, William	22-Nov-1927	5-Oct-1882	New Jersey	103714533	317
Danielson, Peter	28-Apr-1922			103714534	unk
Dappen, Albert	16-Nov-1940	27-Apr-1875	Switzerland	103714535	853
Datzuk, Mike	24-Aug-1948	31-Jan-1887	Russia	103714536	A156
Davenport, Calvin	20-Jan-1948	9-Mar-1877	Texas	103714537	A134
Davidson, Raymond	**30-May-1965**	**2-Dec-1890**	**Michigan**	**60064719**	**A427**
Davis, Benjamin	25-Jul-1937	24-Mar-1893	California	103714538	727
Davis, Charles Henry	18-Dec-1922	5-Dec-1869	Indiana	103714539	unk
Davis, Edwin	4-Mar-1944	9-Jun-1880	Nashville, TN	103714540	987
Davis, Harry	**15-Nov-1967**	**20-Mar-1900**	**California**	**97530433**	**A458**
Davis, Jesse S.	23-Jun-1944	16-Jun-1878	Springfield, MO	102195621	A5
Davis, John L.	4-Aug-1931	30-May-1879	Tennessee	103714541	488
Davis, Melvin Edgar	26-Nov-1937	24-Jan-1881	Oroville, CA	101797551	741
Daws, Harry	26-Oct-1965	28-Mar-1900	Illinois	102322397	A432
Dawson, William	14-May-1931	4-May-1895	Montana	103714542	475
De Campo, Jose Dose	10-Sep-1929	15-Apr-1884	Spain	103714543	398
De Larra, Mary	19-Nov-1938	11-Jun-1908	Steubenville, Iowa	103714544	781
Deal, George	11-Nov-1936	21-Feb-1887	Oregon	103041216	700
Del Bino, Serafino	17-Nov-1926	13-Jul-1882	Italy	103714545	276
Delacruz, Isadore	25-Apr-1926	4-Jun-1899	Philippines	103714546	250
Delacruz, Juan	14-Feb-1930	3-Dec-1884	Mexico	103714547	411

31

Robin Yonash

Name	Birth Date	Birth Location	FAG	Grave
Delgadillo, Diego	1-Jan-1908	Mexico	103714548	803
Demarakis, Demetrius	15-Sep-1877	Greece	103714549	A7
Derivo, Tony	12-Sep-1872	Italy	103714550	A108
Derx, Penrose	11-Jun-1877	Illinois	103714551	A100
Detko, Martnay	1-Oct-1878	Russia	103714552	A407
Devlin, William H.	10-Oct-1874	Pennsylvania	103714553	762
Diaz, Domingo	19-Aug-1903	Mexico	103714554	401
Diaz, Jose	1893	Mexico	103714555	A158
Dickey, William G.	15-Feb-1882	Virginia	103714556	760
Diederich, Joseph L.	25-May-1878	France	103714557	351
Dillon, Jack	14-Jan-1899	Missouri	103714558	604
Dingerson, John	24-Mar-1872	Illinois	103714559	unk
Dixon, Joe	22-Jun-1884	Arkansas	103714560	unk
Dixon, Oliver	19-Jan-1900	Louisiana	103714561	633
Dobbins, Tomas	10-Oct-1869	California	103714562	687
Dodig, John	29-Oct-1884	Austria	103714563	592
Doherty, Patrick	24-May-1864	Ireland	103714564	789
Dominguez, Carlos		Mexico	103714567	618
Dominguez, Gregorio	12-Mar-1902	Mexico	103714568	921
Doputa, Petas	1886	Slavia	103714569	434
Dorsey, Robert	29-Jan-1853	Illinois	103714570	unk
Dougherty, Edward	14-Aug-1882	Ireland	103714571	568

History of the Weimar Joint Sanatorium and the Weimar Cemetery

Name	Death Date	Birth Date	Birth Location	FAG	Grave
Dougherty, Thomas	**14-May-1960**	**31-Jul-1908**	**New Jersey**	**97581066**	**A357**
Dougherty, William	21-Sep-1927	1-Jul-1874	Ireland	103714572	305
Downing, Charles	20-Nov-1926	19-Jan-1878	Oklahoma	33747525	277
Doyle, Patrick	29-Jun-1933	13-Mar-1863	Pennsylvania	103714573	566
Drazich, Robert	14-Oct-1950	24-Mar-1882	Yugoslavia	103714575	A209
Drew, Leroy	9-Jun-1967	25-Aug-1928	Louisiana	103714576	A451
Drew, William	6-Apr-1920	17-Apr-1867	Pennsylvania	103714577	unk
Drummond, Elmer Grant	17-Jan-1920	11-Mar-1864	California	103714578	unk
Duarte, Andres Q.	29-Mar-1961	30-Nov-1890	Mexico	103714579	A371
Duarte, Marcos	30-Jul-1926	25-Apr-1891	Mexico	103714580	263
Duffy, James	4-May-1929	1885	Ireland	103714581	383
Duncan, John	14-Nov-1933	19-Oct-1864	Nevada	103714582	586
Dunlap, Harry	26-Nov-1934	22-Jul-1878	Ohio	103714583	628
Dunn, James	16-Feb-1944	9-Mar-1900	Brooklyn, NY	103714584	984
Duran, Patricio	30-Nov-1961	15-Mar-1866	New Mexico	103714585	A388
Duvas, Joe	15-Apr-1920	19-Mar-1890	Italy	103714586	unk
Earhart, Homer	2-May-1938	16-Jan-1891	Denver, CO	103714587	761
Echeverria, Barbara	21-Jul-1966	13-Jun-1931	Idaho	103714588	A437
Edman, Pete	20-Aug-1925	31-Jan-1890	Sweden	103714589	229
Edwards, Thomas O.	25-Apr-1937	3-Sep-1861	Tennessee	103714590	717
Edwards, William	17-Aug-1939	22-Dec-1871	Alabama	103714591	808
Eilers, Alrich	16-Aug-1947	19-Jun-1872	Germany	103714592	A118

Robin Yonash

Name	Death Date	Birth Date	Birth Location	FAG	Grave
Ellis, Jesse M.	13-Dec-1944	28-Oct-1908	Canton, GA	102252360	A18
Ellis, Lena	25-Jul-1930	15-Apr-1906	Alabama	103714593	427
Enos, Manuel	14-Mar-1925		Portugal	103714594	200
Enquist, Simon	6-Mar-1933	27-Jan-1883	Finland	103714595	553
Erickson, Erick	9-Oct-1933	31-Oct-1885	Finland	103714596	582
Erickson, John	27-Dec-1941	27-Oct-1869	Sweden	103714597	890
Erickson, Vaino	24-Mar-1921	1881	Finland	103714598	unk
Erke, Walter	8-Apr-1948	16-Jul-1895	Wisconsin	103714599	A146
Escobedo, Guadalupe	25-Mar-1929	26-Feb-1913	Mexico	103714600	381
Espersa, Sista	28-Mar-1927	28-Mar-1895	Mexico	103714601	287
Espino, Helen	13-Sep-1937	31-Jan-1921	Mexico	103714602	733
Esquer, Manuel	3-Dec-1932	1888	Mexico	103714603	539
Evans, Robert	5-Jan-1928	2-May-1905	Arkansas	103714604	323
Evans, Ross	27-Feb-1926	14-May-1895	Missouri	103714606	245
Eyhour, Otto	26-Jul-1920	28-Dec-1880		103714607	unk
Facio, Antonio	8-Jul-1955	22-Oct-1898	Mexico	103714608	A265
Factora, Moises D.	16-Jan-1946	25-May-1902	Philippines	103714609	A57
Fahey, John	27-Oct-1940	16-Aug-1892	Newfoundland	103714610	851
Farr, John L.	6-Mar-1931	4-Feb-1904	Georgia	103714611	460
Farrell, Florence	20-May-1960	2-Dec-1905	Minnesota	103714612	A359
Fatich, Steve	23-Oct-1936	Oct-1875	Serbia	103714613	697
Fedrigo, Joseph	29-Sep-1922	19-May-1888	Italy	103714614	unk

34

History of the Weimar Joint Sanatorium and the Weimar Cemetery

Name	Death Date	Birth Date	Birth Location	FAG	Grave
Fenton, John	15-Dec-1936	10-Mar-1890	Wales	103714615	707
Fenton, Norman	9-Aug-1963	29-Dec-1900	Omaha, NE	103714616	A408
Fernandez, Fred	1-Sep-1955	18-Jul-1900	Mexico	103714617	A268
Fernandez, Jesus	13-Feb-1936	22-Dec-1849	Mexico	103714618	678
Fernandez, Thomas	29-Apr-1944	13-Aug-1895	Spain	103714619	994
Ferreira, Antonio	6-Jul-1924	23-Jan-1885	Portugal	103714620	162
Fetty, Wallace	21-Nov-1970	10-Apr-1932	Kansas	102323376	A471
Field, Frank	16-Apr-1967	5-May-1906	Missouri	103714621	A449
Fierras, Frederico	29-Nov-1938		Mexico	103714622	783
Figaro, Nicholas	30-Nov-1943	15-Nov-1880	Italy	103714623	971
Finch, William	7-Jul-1934	15-May-1862	Michigan	103714624	610
Fioretto, Angelo	8-Jul-1928	3-Jul-1878	Italy	103714625	348
Firkus, Louis J.	16-Mar-1931	30-Oct-1883	Wisconsin	101806449	462
Fischer, Herman	4-Nov-1967	1-Apr-1884	Russia	103714626	A457
Fisher, Frank Paul	9-Jan-1924	12-Nov-1862	Pennsylvania	103714627	137
Fisher, James	4-Oct-1966	4-Jul-1920	Illinois	103714628	A442
Fisher, Rollie	2-Feb-1939	13-Jul-1886	Missouri	103714629	788
Fitzgerald, William B.	8-Dec-1932	18-Apr-1883	Nebraska	103714630	542
Flanagan, William	24-Oct-1944	10-Sep-1882	Glouchester City, NJ	103714631	A13
Flavio, Canalez	21-May-1925	7-May-1900	Mexico	103714632	209
Flood, Harry	5-Jun-1929	14-Feb-1875	Missouri	103714633	386
Flood, Theodore	10-Apr-1921	25-Sep-1860	California	103714634	unk

35

Name	Death Date	Birth Date	Birth Location	FAG	Grave
Flores, Bennie D.	**22-Mar-1956**	**15-Jan-1904**	**Hawaii**	**97530758**	**A283**
Flores, Jose	2-Aug-1927	Mar-1882	Mexico	103714635	298
Flores, Jose	18-Oct-1932	Mar-1892	Mexico	103714636	532
Florez, Frank H.	30-Dec-1940	4-Sep-1904	Mexico	103714637	863
Flynn, Martin	14-Jan-1921	9-Apr-1870	Canada	103714639	unk
Fonseca, Juan	10-Apr-1961		Mexico	103714640	A372
Forkell, Edward	**14-Aug-1956**	**9-Jan-1891**	**New York**	**97465935**	**A292**
Foster, Francis	18-May-1943	11-Oct-1901	Jennings, KS	103714641	948
Foster, John W.	12-May-1920	20-Dec-1860	Illinois	101804684	unk
Foster, Joseph	8-Jun-1939	17-Mar-1883	Depauw, Indiana	103714642	800
Fowler, George W.	31-Oct-1945	6-Feb-1904	Bristow, OK	103714643	A51
Frain, George	12-Nov-1970	24-Sep-1883	California	103714644	A470
Frames, Tom	26-Feb-1933	1885	Greece	103714645	552
Franklin, A. K.	16-Jun-1924	22-Oct-1879	Texas	103714646	159
Franklin, Harry	3-Oct-1936	6-Dec-1882	Iowa	103714647	695
Freeland, Carl	26-Feb-1924	1-Mar-1889	Oregon	103714648	141
Freeland, James	1-Apr-1937	20-Nov-1875	North Carolina	103714649	716
Freeman, McKinley	7-Mar-1924	1-Mar-1900	Texas	103714650	143
Freese, Al E.	24-Sep-1926	8-Feb-1904	Missouri	103714651	270
Frezzini, John	14-Nov-1942	24-Jun-1896	Italy	103714652	916
Frias, Joe	7-Jul-1932	24-Apr-1896	Philippines	103714653	522
Frizihara, Masuichi	26-Aug-1929	29-Nov-1881	Japan	103714654	397

36

History of the Weimar Joint Sanatorium and the Weimar Cemetery

Name	Death Date	Birth Date	Birth Location	FAG	Grave
Frontas, Arturo	16-Jun-1933	30-Mar-1895	Spain	103714655	564
Fuentes, Gilbert	25-Apr-1925	1893	Mexico	103714656	206
Gaddi, Fred	9-Dec-1924	6-Feb-1878	Italy	103714657	183
Galarza, Ynez	16-Oct-1959	27-Dec-1899	Mexico	103714658	A348
Galis, Oscar	3-Dec-1924	6-Feb-1898	Georgia	103714659	180
Gallagher, Frank	13-Mar-1922	18-Dec-1881	Tennessee	103714660	unk
Galloway, Joseph M.	6-May-1943	5-Jun-1874	St. Louis, MO	103714661	945
Garay, Mariano	22-Mar-1948	1897	Mexico	103714662	A143
Garcia, Adeline	5-Aug-1927	10-Mar-1904	Colorado	103714663	299
Garcia, Benito	21-Sep-1930	1880	Mexico	103714664	440
Garcia, Ciapiano	29-Dec-1937	16-Jan-1880	Spain	103714665	744
Garcia, Frank	6-Apr-1925	1900	Mexico	103714667	203
Garcia, Frank	10-Jun-1954	19-Jan-1905	Silao, Mexico	103714666	A255
Garcia, Jesse	16-Jan-1924		New Mexico	103714668	138
Garcia, Jesus Soto	28-Jul-1945	18-Jun-1897	Mexico	103714669	A43
Garcia, John Diaz	6-Jun-1940	29-Aug-1909	Mexico	103714670	838
Garcia, Jose	6-Jul-1925	13-Feb-1892	Mexico	103714671	215
Garcia, Joseph	29-Jan-1937	Dec-1927	California	103714672	709
Garcia, Juan	21-Jun-1934	24-Jun-1907	New Mexico	99270567	609
Garcia, Lupe	22-May-1939	31-May-1912	El Paso, TX	103714673	797
Garcia, Mary	22-Mar-1929	22-Sep-1916	California	103714674	378
Garcia, Preciliano	7-Aug-1929	19-Oct-1909	Mexico	103714675	392

Robin Yonash

Name	Death Date	Birth Date	Birth Location	FAG	Grave
Garcia, Rumaldo	20-Sep-1964	7-Feb-1905	Texas	103714676	A420
Garduno, Leon	11-Apr-1924	28-Jun-1902	Mexico	103714677	148
Garjola, Emery	2-Dec-1932	13-Apr-1912	Texas	103714678	537
Gauthier, Peter	**16-Jan-1955**	**4-Nov-1907**	**New York**	**97470481**	**A261**
Gavigan, John	28-Sep-1932	1865	Indiana	103714679	529
Gayo, Ben	14-Aug-1959	30-Apr-1890	Spain	103714680	A346
Gayovich, Sam	29-Jan-1943	15-May-1888	Yugoslavia	103714681	929
Gaytan, Manuel	29-Apr-1956	20-Feb-1901	Mexico	103714682	A288
Genos, Harry	2-Apr-1935	20-Dec-1882	Greece	103714683	644
Geraldez, Conrado	26-Jan-1929	22-Jun-1901	Philippines	103714684	375
Geron, Estanislaus	2-Aug-1932	7-May-1890	New Mexico	103714685	525
Gilbertsen, Edgar	27-Jul-1937	22-Sep-1894	North Dakota	103714686	729
Gilchrist, Robert	10-Sep-1926	13-Sep-1883	Scotland	103714687	269
Gilchrist, William	31-Jan-1947	2-Dec-1893	California	103714688	A89
Gill, John	29-Sep-1925	2-Feb-1873	Pennsylvania	103714689	231
Gipe, Charles	19-Apr-1936	9-Apr-1867	California	103714690	681
Giraldi, Louis	15-Jan-1931	31-Mar-1880	Italy	103714691	452
Girardi, Therese	12-Dec-1924	5-May-1899	France	103714692	184
Girevara, Vera	24-Aug-1931	27-Apr-1927	California	103714693	492
Girod, Albert	17-Jul-1959	14-Mar-1898	Switzerland	103714694	A345
Gleason, James	16-Jan-1922	4-Mar-1872	Maryland	103714695	unk
Gobi, Eugenio	6-Jul-1927	8-Mar-1888	Italy	103714696	294

38

History of the Weimar Joint Sanatorium and the Weimar Cemetery

Name	Death Date	Birth Date	Birth Location	FAG	Grave
Goggins, Maurice	28-May-1935	1-Nov-1874	Ireland	103714697	652
Gomez, Antonio	17-Aug-1960	13-Apr-1880	Mexico	103714698	A362
Gomez, Benita	31-Jul-1933	21-Mar-1913	Mexico	103714699	572
Gonsales, Frank	21-Jul-1958	24-Jun-1903	Mexico	103714700	A330
Gonsales, Guadalupe	14-Apr-1921	1888	Mexico	103714701	unk
Gonzales, Thomas	23-Feb-1940	7-Mar-1904	Santa Fe, NM	103714702	822
Gonzalez, Antonio	22-Jun-1921	9-Jun-1888	Spain	103714703	unk
Gonzalez, Carlos	4-Feb-1945	6-Apr-1914	Mexico	103714704	A24
Gonzalez, Maria	23-Jun-1921	24-Nov-1903	Texas	103714705	unk
Gonzalez, Pedro	31-May-1944	29-Jun-1888	Mexico	103714706	1000
Gonzalez, Percy	6-Oct-1922	8-Dec-1884	Mexico	103714707	unk
Good, Frank	18-May-1926	14-Nov-1884	California	103714708	255
Gooding, Fred Amos	1-Jan-1924	15-Jul-1868	Massachusetts	103714709	135
Goodwin, William S.	24-Dec-1934	27-Feb-1862	Kentucky	103714710	632
Gordon, John	13-Feb-1935	12-Oct-1863	Mexico	103714711	639
Gotti, Antone	15-Oct-1933	18-Feb-1890	Italy	103714712	583
Gould, Harold, J.	12-Mar-1959	28-Oct-1887	Canada	103714713	A343
Graham, Robert	21-Jul-1930	1-Mar-1877	California	103714714	425
Graham, William Joseph	7-Oct-1927	9-Dec-1882	Illinois	103714715	307
Grainger, Elvis	29-Jan-1935	1-Jan-1899	California	103714716	635
Grant, Lena	20-Feb-1944	23-May-1888	Burney, CA	103714717	986
Grant, Owen	23-Jul-1930	15-Jul-1896	Ireland	103714718	426

39

Robin Yonash

Name	Death Date	Birth Date	Birth Location	FAG	Grave
Grbac, George	5-Jun-1935	15-May-1893	Yugoslavia	103714719	654
Green, Bill Harry	7-Nov-1958	1-Aug-1888	Bald Hill, PA	103714720	A337
Greenway, William	28-Nov-1925	7-Jun-1874	Ireland	103714721	240
Gregg, Frank	14-Nov-1938	10-May-1871	Oklahoma	103714723	780
Gregory, Bert	21-Dec-1934	10-May-1904	Montana	103714724	631
Guerro, Antonia	27-Feb-1938	13-Feb-1925	Sacramento, CA	103714725	757
Guiliani, Antonio	7-Dec-1932	24-Jun-1891	Italy	103714726	541
Guirado, Pedro	16-Jun-1926	1897	Mexico	103714727	259
Gumbleton, Lawrence	28-Jun-1948	24-Jan-1899	Maine	103714728	A152
Gutierrez, Antonio	24-Apr-1932	11-Feb-1882	California	103714729	517
Gutierrez, Benitos Juan Antonio	11-Oct-1946	22-Mar-1898	Spain	103714730	A77
Gutierrez, Crecencio	17-Oct-1930	15-Jul-1904	Mexico	103714733	444
Gutierrez, Jose	24-Feb-1956	19-Mar-1899	Mexico	103714734	A279
Gutierrez, Paul	18-Apr-1934	13-Jan-1903	Mexico	103714735	603
Guzman, Jose	10-May-1949	1-May-1908	Mexico	103714736	A183
Hackett, William R.	17-Apr-1926	13-Sep-1879	Kentucky	103714737	249
Haley, William	14-Mar-1920	7-Feb-1850		103714738	unk
Hall, Elsie	4-Jan-1950	29-Nov-1915	Arkansas	103714739	A196
Hallenborg, Frances	5-Jul-1948	19-Jun-1911	Nebraska	103084986	A153
Hallenborg, Roy V .	**10-Dec-1951**	**8-Nov-1897**	**Nebraska**	**60064912**	**A225**
Halpin, Joseph	9-Jan-1933	17-Apr-1881	San Francisco, CA	103714740	546
Hansen, Charles	11-Mar-1928	2-May-1889	Washington	103714741	333

History of the Weimar Joint Sanatorium and the Weimar Cemetery

Name	Death Date	Birth Date	Birth Location	FAG	Grave
Hansen, George	29-Jan-1944	6-Jun-1883	Denmark	103714742	981
Hansen, Walter	27-Jan-1928	14-Apr-1886	Wisconsin	103714743	327
Hanson, Barney	24-Jul-1937	30-Jan-1891	Oregon	103714744	726
Hanson, Frank	5-Aug-1957	28-Dec-1905	Tacoma, WA	102318430	A313
Hanson, Peter	11-Mar-1923	17-Nov-1887	Sweden	103714745	unk
Hardie, Jackson	12-Jul-1925	Sep-1867	Illinois	103714746	217
Harger, Thurmon	22-Aug-1934	11-Aug-1902	Oklahoma	99271333	615
Harmon, Jacob	1-Feb-1951	11-Nov-1896	Russia	103714747	A215
Harp, Walter	9-Sep-1951	12-Apr-1901	Scipio, OK	102317262	A222
Harris, Charles	2-Oct-1963	13-Jul-1904	England	103714748	A411
Harris, John	3-Nov-1920	30-Oct-1876	England	103714749	unk
Harris, Thomas	11-Feb-1920	14-Jun-1852	England	103714750	unk
Harrison, Belle	20-Jan-1920	21-Feb-1891	Kentucky	95546049	unk
Harrison, Edward	26-Jul-1945	18-Nov-1885	Mt. Carmel, IL	102279476	A41
Harrison, Henry	28-Dec-1957	8-Jul-1878	Massachusetts	103714751	A321
Hartman, Ralph	20-Jan-1942	18-Aug-1884	Chico, CA	102236501	893
Harvey, Clifford	24-Feb-1924	28-Dec-1899	California	103714752	140
Harvey, James	2-Sep-1921	26-Jun-1876	Australia	103714753	unk
Hasegawa, Eizo	5-Sep-1947	15-Apr-1877	Japan	103714754	A124
Haskell, Harry	3-Sep-1963	23-Aug-1899	Wisconsin	103714755	A409
Hattery, John	12-Jun-1944	16-Dec-1882	Ventura, CA	103714757	A4
Hayes, Edward Elvin	9-Dec-1955	19-Sep-1912	Lima, Ohio	103714758	A274

41

Name	Death Date	Birth Date	Birth Location	FAG	Grave
Hazelwood, Claude	31-Aug-1930	15-Apr-1864	Illinois	103714759	435
Heairelson, Wallace L.	6-Jun-1936	11-May-1884	Texas	103714760	684
Heaney, Mike	18-Oct-1921	7-May-1876	Ireland	103714761	unk
Henderson, Edward	2-May-1940	2-Jan-1877	Vallejo, CA	103041604	828
Hendry, Frank	**15-Aug-1964**	**26-Sep-1899**	**Minnesota**	**97582234**	**A418**
Heredia, Micayle	2-Apr-1931	1895	Mexico	103714762	467
Hernandes, Maria	1-Jun-1926	1896	Mexico	103714763	256
Hernandez, Albert Lopez	19-Mar-1940	6-Oct-1918	Los Angeles, CA	103714764	826
Hernandez, Augustine	14-Jun-1938	28-Aug-1907	Mexico	103714765	769
Hernandez, Jose	29-Sep-1943	19-Mar-1897	El Paso, TX	103714766	967
Hernandez, Reyes	4-Aug-1928	1897	Mexico	103714767	352
Hernandez, Secundino	20-Jul-1943	Jul-1873	Mexico	103714768	956
Hernandez, Trinidad	12-Jul-1928	9-Jul-1909	Texas	103714769	349
Herndon, George James	17-Aug-1942	13-Feb-1881	Tulare Co., CA	102237073	911
Heronaka, Jutaro	12-Aug-1929	3-Oct-1875	Japan	103714770	395
Herrera, Gilbert	21-Mar-1964	4-Feb-1903	Mexico	103714771	A415
Hickman, Walter	19-Sep-1937	21-May-1883	Iowa	103714772	735
Hicks, James	26-Mar-1948	18-Sep-1880	Virginia	103714773	A145
Hicks, Jesse Harvey	16-Oct-1952	6-Feb-1887	Nevada	60064826	A234
Hidalgo, Jose	11-Mar-1953	19-Mar-1898	Mexico	103714774	A240
Hidalgo, Juan	26-Jul-1926	6-May-1880	Spain	103714775	262
Hidalgo, Santiago	13-Aug-1926	7-Jan-1888	Spain	103714776	265

Name	Death Date	Birth Date	Birth Location	FAG	Grave
Hill, Otto	9-Sep-1930	3-Jan-1878	Finland	103714777	439
Hinds, Barney Alvin	17-Feb-1948	29-Sep-1879	Illinois	102315849	A138
Hirschcorn, Emanuel	3-Apr-1956	24-Feb-1891	Russia	103714779	A284
Hitchcock, Rhoda	20-May-1924	12-Sep-1881	Chile	103714780	155
Hodge, Alvin R.	1-Nov-1942	2-Oct-1918	Eagle River, WI	94672682	915
Hoffman, Carl	17-Jun-1931	31-Oct-1869	Germany	103714781	483
Hoffman, Edward	15-Jan-1938	7-Aug-1886	Missouri	103714782	747
Hoffman, John	29-Jul-1966	5-Jun-1884	Austria	103714783	A438
Holland, Charles	**23-Dec-1961**	**29-Mar-1884**	**Oklahoma**	**97471652**	**A391**
Holm, Andy	5-Nov-1923	16-Jun-1870	Sweden	103714784	129
Holm, Gus	18-Oct-1936	1-Nov-1891	Finland	103714785	696
Holquin, Lasara	2-Apr-1922	19-Apr-1891	New Mexico	103714786	unk
Holt, Robert Lanier	6-Feb-1960	24-Aug-1907	South Carolina	103714787	A354
Hom, Check	30-Dec-1948	17-May-1879	China	103714788	A172
Hooker, Homer	30-Jan-1947	11-Oct-1882	Texas	102281091	A88
Horne, Howard	31-Oct-1933	24-Jul-1899	Oklahoma	103714789	585
Horner, John	9-Jan-1955	1-Jun-1879	Pennsylvania	103714790	A260
Horton, St. Elmo	29-Oct-1926	12-Nov-1892	Kentucky	103714791	275
Horton, Willie	30-Apr-1967	6-Sep-1906	Oklahoma	103714792	A450
Houston, Ray	19-Dec-1970	6-Jul-1912	Kansas	103714793	A472
Hovila, Archie	**17-Jul-1949**	**9-Feb-1909**	**Michigan**	**97487287**	**A185**
Howard, William A.	6-Mar-1935	17-Jan-1873	Michigan	103714794	642

43

Robin Yonash

Name	Death Date	Birth Date	Birth Location	FAG	Grave
Huber, Walter	29-Jul-1939	26-Apr-1914	Lowry, SD	103714795	807
Hudolin, Louis	26-Apr-1949	15-Jul-1888	Austria	103714796	A182
Huff, William J.	27-Aug-1935	13-Jun-1900	Iowa	103714797	662
Hughes, Edwin	29-Apr-1921	6-Aug-1870	New York	103714798	unk
Humer, Frank	12-Mar-1949	7-Apr-1887	Ohio	103714799	A177
Hunter, Alexander	2-Jun-1940	3-Mar-1886	Canada	103714800	836
Ichijyo, Kuranosuke K.	5-May-1940	6-Jun-1878	Japan	103714801	829
Ikkela, Ludwig	19-Nov-1939	15-Jan-1884	Finland	103714802	816
Imogean, Frank	5-Jan-1934	13-Mar-1861	Georgia	103714803	590
Ingram, Robert	15-Jun-1940	24-Jan-1884	Trinity Co., CA	103714804	840
Inouye, Yoshiro George	13-May-1944	23-Dec-1903	Japan	103714805	997
Irish, Omer Gilbert	12-Feb-1927	22-Aug-1871	Minnesota	101806111	283
Irwin, William H.	12-Aug-1926	8-Jul-1860	Michigan	103714806	264
Jackson, Lucille	26-Jun-1945	11-Nov-1913	Alexandria, LA	103714807	A39
Jackson, Simon	3-Apr-1947	16-Jan-1909	Oklahoma	103714808	A98
Jackson, Thomas	21-Aug-1928	16-Mar-1848	England	103714809	355
Jacobsen, Axel	13-Jul-1938	30-Oct-1885	Sweden	103714810	771
Jacobson, Alfred	4-Jan-1929	2-Feb-1868	Sweden	103714811	372
Jacoby, Owen Clifford	10-Aug-1940	1-Feb-1884	Nebraska	102231301	843
Jafemann, Charles	5-Feb-1921	18-Aug-1881	California	103714812	unk
James, Alice	19-Oct-1948	14-Sep-1924	Nevada	103714813	A164
Jamison, Rodney Colby	23-Jun-1941	6-Apr-1877	Lake Co., CA	102233167	876

44

History of the Weimar Joint Sanatorium and the Weimar Cemetery

Name	Death Date	Birth Date	Birth Location	FAG	Grave
Jaricow, Fred	8-Jun-1938	27-Sep-1882	Russia	103714814	768
Jayo, Juan	31-May-1948	29-Nov-1884	Spain	103714815	A149
Jenkin, Gertrude	7-Oct-1966	17-Dec-1870	England	103714816	A443
Jenkins, Russell	21-Jul-1921	6-Aug-1885	Indiana	102195408	unk
Jenkinson, Henry	24-Jan-1947	29-Dec-1885	England	103714817	A91
Jensen, Adolph	15-Sep-1942	17-Dec-1882	Denmark	103714819	913
Jensen, Hans Johannis	5-Jan-1945	4-Jul-1873	Denmark	103714820	A21
Jewett, Charles	23-Sep-1922	14-Apr-1865	California	103714821	unk
Jimenez, Joe	24-May-1940	13-Jul-1918	Santa Rita, NM	30277313	835
Jimenez, Juan	30-Jan-1963	22-Jun-1898	Mexico	103714822	A401
Joe, King	7-Aug-1949	15-Feb-1893	California	103714823	A187
Johns, Lee	4-Jan-1947	12-Jan-1882	Pennsylvania	103714824	A84
Johns, William H.	28-Aug-1928	26-Jun-1882	Massachusetts	103714825	358
Johnson, August J.	27-Jun-1923	9-Feb-1868	Tennessee	103714826	120
Johnson, Charles	30-May-1927	31-Jan-1887	Finland	103714830	289
Johnson, Charles	30-Oct-1927	23-Dec-1862	Sweden	103714828	314
Johnson, Charles	27-Aug-1928	6-Jun-1857	Sweden	103714827	357
Johnson, Charles	14-Aug-1930	22-Jan-1894	Norway	103714829	431
Johnson, Emil	22-Dec-1943	15-Jun-1888	Finland	103714831	973
Johnson, Guy	15-May-1944	16-Apr-1912	Atlanta, GA	103714832	998
Johnson, Lena	26-Jun-1957	29-Feb-1924	Alabama	103714833	A312
Johnson, M. J.	13-Feb-1945	3-Dec-1897	Bastrop, LA	103714834	A28

Name	Death Date	Birth Date	Birth Location	FAG	Grave
Johnson, Phillip	**24-Jul-1948**	**20-May-1919**	**Pennsylvania**	**97530995**	**A155**
Johnson, Swan	22-Oct-1925	8-Apr-1874	Sweden	103714835	234
Johnson, Victor	27-Jul-1937	10-Aug-1855	Sweden	103714836	728
Johnson, Victor	1-Jan-1944	5-Mar-1879	Sweden	103714837	975
Johnson, William	4-Sep-1924	3-Nov-1877	Pennsylvania	103714839	166
Johnson, William	2-Dec-1936	6-Apr-1875	England	103714838	702
Johnson, William A.	9-Aug-1923	14-Aug-1876	California	103714840	124
Jones, Claude	31-Jul-1961	8-Jan-1905	Texas	103714841	A378
Jones, Floyd	28-Apr-1960	24-Oct-1915	North Dakota	103714842	A356
Jones, Herbert Lee	1-Mar-1964	17-Jul-1913	Texas	103714843	A414
Jones, John Henry	30-Jun-1942	22-Dec-1893	Kendrick, Idaho	103714844	903
Jones, Robert	10-Jun-1930	11-Aug-1860	Wales	103714845	420
Jones, Thelma Mae	13-Dec-1945	16-Jul-1922	Martinez, CA	103714846	A54
Joo, Y. S.	6-Apr-1927	12-May-1873	Korea	103714847	284
Jordan, John	22-Nov-1927	6-Nov-1885	Ohio	101806263	316
Juarez, Rodolfo	14-Jul-1948	16-Dec-1914	Mexico	103714848	A154
Jukich, Rade	5-Oct-1935	6-Dec-1894	Unknown	103714849	665
Kahn, Heder Ali	8-Apr-1939	1899	India	103714850	794
Kalama, Martin	18-Dec-1952	22-Oct-1900	Hawaii	103714851	A236
Kalan, John H.	20-Apr-1944	1-Jun-1890	Austria	103714853	993
Kalifa, Mohamid	19-Jun-1958	20-Mar-1879	Tunisia	103714854	A329
Kamensky, Alexander	**1-Oct-1946**	**7-Mar-1897**	**Poland**	**97518527**	**A76**

Name	Death Date	Birth Date	Birth Location	FAG	Grave
Kane, John	21-Sep-1936	26-Jun-1879	Pennsylvania	103714856	694
Kane, William Andy	15-Jun-1934	19-Mar-1893	Michigan	103714857	608
Karaga, Luy	31-Aug-1956	18-Oct-1889	Austria	103714858	A294
Kataoka, Tsutaichro	16-Apr-1941	8-Feb-1880	Japan	103714859	870
Katsandonis, John	13-Nov-1957	26-Oct-1888	Greece	103714860	A320
Kauffman, Richard Diptson	30-Aug-1947	4-Dec-1880	Pennsylvania	103714861	A122
Kavouras, Sam	31-Dec-1928	8-Aug-1900	Greece	103714862	371
Kaylor, Bernard B.	22-Aug-1931	16-Apr-1870	Ohio	103714863	491
Kazanegra, Marko	20-Mar-1924	25-Jul-1883	Serbia	103714864	145
Keast, Fred	9-Jul-1934	4-Jul-1874	Michigan	103714865	611
Keelan, Jack	31-Jul-1942	2-Mar-1896	Scotland	103714866	906
Keller, James Frank	8-Jun-1951	10-Jan-1884	Missouri	103714867	A220
Kelley, Bert Craig	14-Oct-1953	23-Apr-1882	Moline, IL	103714868	A245
Kelley, James	**18-Feb-1922**	**13-Jan-1873**	**Ireland**	**103714869**	**unk**
Kelly, Burrell Elmer	10-Dec-1936	1903	California	103714870	704
Kelly, Frank	28-Feb-1925	14-Jan-1873	Iowa	103714871	198
Kelly, James	14-Apr-1958	16-Nov-1882	England	97517064	A324
Kelly, John Joseph	**3-Sep-1967**	**22-Mar-1890**	**Ireland**	**97529931**	**A454**
Kelly, Thomas Howard	18-Aug-1956	16-Sep-1905	New York	103714872	A293
Kelso, John	23-May-1924	3-Aug-1879	New Jersey	103714873	156
Kemp, Samuel	3-Jan-1971	1-Feb-1892	England	103714874	A473
Kernan, Philip	9-Oct-1923	10-Jan-1863	Maryland	103714875	127

47

Robin Yonash

Name	Death Date	Birth Date	Birth Location	FAG	Grave
Ketchersid, Thomas R.	31-Jan-1943	1-May-1894	Waco, TX	102249779	930
Khan, Murtazan	22-Apr-1957	1-Jan-1884	Canamel, India	103714876	A310
Kidd, Theodore R.	31-Oct-1957	27-Nov-1907	Oklahoma	102319567	A318
Kidd, William	26-Sep-1967	10-Feb-1900	Mississippi	103714877	A456
Kindel, William	22-Oct-1947	12-Mar-1891	Pennsylvania	103714878	A130
King, Ed	2-Aug-1958	1-Aug-1910	Houston, TX	103714879	A332
King, Guy Edward	1-Mar-1948	21-Nov-1900	Ohio	103714880	A140
King, James Elmer	16-May-1954	7-Feb-1875	Missouri	103714881	A253
King, John	4-Jan-1936	25-Dec-1898	California	103714882	676
King, Robert	9-Feb-1947	20-Oct-1907	Louisana	103714883	A93
King, Thomas	5-Mar-1922	24-Mar-1861	Massachusetts	103714884	unk
Kingsbury, Theodore	29-Sep-1938	11-Nov-1868	Yankton, SD	103714885	776
Kinoshita, Naokichi	20-Jul-1940	15-Mar-1870	Japan	103714886	842
Kirchner, William G.	11-Oct-1945	21-Nov-1899	Douglas, WA	102280059	A47
Kitagawa, Yusoburo	23-Dec-1950	25-Nov-1874	Japan	103714887	A212
Kitchmar, Albert	25-Oct-1930	Apr-1885	Nebraska	103714888	445
Klasna, Dan	20-Jul-1929	27-Jan-1884	Yugoslavia	103714889	390
Klegg, Frank	17-Apr-1931	22-Jul-1882	Bohemia	103714890	471
Klein, Albert M.	27-Sep-1945	15-Feb-1885	Chicago, IL	103714891	A46
Kline, Richard	20-Dec-1927	30-Nov-1871	California	103714892	319
Knowles, Wallace	17-Jan-1956	18-Mar-1888	San Francisco, CA	103714893	A275
Kolzen, William Edward	4-Aug-1946	16-Apr-1916	Illinois	102280520	A74

48

History of the Weimar Joint Sanatorium and the Weimar Cemetery

Name	Death Date	Birth Date	Birth Location	FAG	Grave
Koontz, Howard	26-May-1957	3-Jan-1897	Charleston, W. Va.	103714894	A311
Kovachevich, Dave	3-Aug-1930	20-Jun-1877	Austria	103714895	428
Kovacovich, Chris	26-Aug-1924	28-Mar-1885	Montenegro	103714896	165
Koyanagi, Isematsu	27-Apr-1943	28-Nov-1881	Japan	103714896	943
Kroll, Frank	25-Apr-1946	4-Jun-1896	Illinois	103714898	A66
Kufren, Frank	2-Jun-1945	25-Jul-1896	Yugoslavia	103714899	A36
Kukuljan, Baldo	8-Oct-1950	26-Jan-1892	Yugoslavia	103714900	A208
Kummer, Ernest	1-Nov-1936	9-Jul-1888	Germany	103714901	698
Lacey, Victor	16-Dec-1924	16-Aug-1883	Austria	103714902	185
LaChance, Frank	10-Jun-1927	13-Oct-1873	Minnesota	103714903	292
Ladukis, Tony	24-Oct-1933	17-Jan-1888	Greece	103714904	584
LaForest, Earl	15-Dec-1949	14-Sep-1885	Indiana	103714905	A193
Lai, Look	17-Oct-1927	7-Mar-1864	China	103714906	310
Lamont, Fred	16-Oct-1921	8-Oct-1884	Canada	103714907	unk
Lara, Cipriano C.	25-Jan-1954	16-Sep-1904	Mexico	103714908	A248
LaRose, Steven	18-Sep-1931	22-Dec-1880	Mexico	103714909	496
Larson, John	8-Dec-1929	3-Jul-1881	Finland	103714910	405
Larson, Mike	14-Feb-1928	21-Jan-1884	Finland	103714911	331
LaRue, Herbert John	14-Feb-1943	26-Nov-1890	San Francisco, CA	103714912	932
Laskowski, Frank	20-Apr-1946	17-Sep-1899	Ohio	103714913	A63
Lavandaro, Joe	19-Sep-1922	21-Feb-1885	Spain	103714914	unk
Lavideo, James	4-Dec-1932	26-Jun-1874	Greece	103714916	540

49

Robin Yonash

Name	Death Date	Birth Date	Birth Location	FAG	Grave
Lavin, Jesus	6-May-1940	25-Jan-1892	Spain	103714917	830
Bob, Lawrence	5-Feb-1938	17-Apr-1920	Greenville, CA	103714918	754
LeClair, Wallace	3-Oct-1948	5-Apr-1888	Oregon	102316361	A163
Lee, Earl	27-Sep-1947	30-Nov-1886	Colorado	103714919	A126
Lee, Edwin	4-Mar-1942	15-Oct-1910	Courtland, CA	103714920	896
Lee, Joe	10-Dec-1940	9-Sep-1902	China	103714921	859
Lee, Young—See Marks, Yung					
LeMay, Charles E.	27-Jan-1931	24-Feb-1865	Indiana	103714922	454
Lenihan, Malachy	23-Jan-1939	Dec-1871	Italy	103714923	786
Lennon, John Edward	3-Jun-1940	24-Dec-1877	Connecticut	103714924	837
Leon, Reyes	23-Mar-1943	14-Sep-1922	La Habra, CA	103714925	938
Leonard, Jack	6-Jun-1931	1892	Michigan	103714926	478
Leonard, James E.	7-Jun-1928	5-Nov-1890	Ohio	103714927	344
Leong, Chock	23-Mar-1966	4-Mar-1885	China	8808513	A434
Lerma, Ernest	15-Feb-1930	26-Feb-1906	Mexico	103714928	413
Lester, Fred	13-Feb-1949	28-Jan-1879	New York	103714929	A174
Lewis, Charles J.	26-Jul-1923	19-Aug-1891	Illinois	103714930	123
Lewis, Harry	5-Aug-1928	Oct-1882	California	103714931	353
Lewis, Henry	**14-Oct-1943**	**18-Oct-1904**	**Pearson, MS**	**103714932**	**969**
Lewis, Madeline	19-Nov-1924	29-Nov-1897	California	103714933	177
Ligasen, Guillermo	24-May-1941	5-Sep-1909	Philippines	103714934	871
Lincoln, Darrell	6-Apr-1967	3-Mar-1916	California	103714935	A448

50

History of the Weimar Joint Sanatorium and the Weimar Cemetery

Name	Death Date	Birth Date	Birth Location	FAG	Grave
Lind, Charles	24-Mar-1923	28-Jun-1866	Sweden	103714936	unk
Lindberg, Edward	2-Nov-1966	17-Sep-1901	Kansas	103714937	A445
Lira, Torbis	22-Nov-1936	17-Apr-1878	Mexico	103714938	701
Lloyd, Harry	11-Aug-1935	27-Oct-1864	Pennsylvania	103714958	659
Loder, Aaron	16-May-1940	2-Jan-1902	Lincoln, NE	103714939	833
Logan, Freddie Lee	19-Oct-1945	2-May-1922	Columbia, MO	103714940	A48
Lomas, Norma Alice	30-Jan-1950	26-Jun-1948	California	103714941	A198
Lonergan, William	18-Sep-1948	26-Nov-1892	Connecticut	103714942	A157
Long, Nestor	23-Jun-1939	28-Sep-1893	Finland	103714943	801
Lopez, Benigno	19-Feb-1948	19-Feb-1907	Mexico	103714944	A139
Lopez, Cyrus	5-Dec-1940	28-Jun-1886	Troy, Indiana	99519469	857
Lopez, Donaciano	5-Oct-1961	17-May-1875	Mexico	103714945	A382
Lopez, Doris	1-Feb-1938	14-Jun-1922	California	103714946	752
Lopez, Frank B.	1-Dec-1924	1879	Spain	103714947	179
Lopez, Juan	22-Nov-1942	25-Jun-1887	Mexico	103714948	918
Lopez, Juan	25-Dec-1950	24-Aug-1905	Spain	103714949	A213
Lopez, Lucas	11-Nov-1938	27-Sep-1897	Mexico	103714950	778
Lopez, Manuel	5-Dec-1943	31-May-1888	Portugal	103714953	972
Lopez, Roy	30-Oct-1926	9-Jan-1886	Spain	98172030	274
Losey, Stanley	24-Jun-1947	4-Sep-1892	Ohio	103714954	A109
Louie, Jan	14-Nov-1938	2-Feb-1914	China	103714955	779
Louth, Walter	23-Jan-1954	25-Aug-1888	Ohio	102318162	A247

51

Robin Yonash

Name	Death Date	Birth Date	Birth Location	FAG	Grave
Lovell, Victor R.	22-Sep-1967	20-Nov-1911	North Dakota	103714956	A455
Lowery, Jack	23-Sep-1964	11-Feb-1916	Oklahoma	103714957	A421
Lozano, Leandro	3-May-1937	18-Feb-1920	Mexico	103714960	718
Lubich, John	30-Nov-1940	15-Sep-1893	Leadville, CO	103714961	856
Lucchesi, Angelo	24-Sep-1933	15-May-1878	Italy	103714962	579
Lugo, Ignacio	23-Jun-1944	1-Feb-1903	Mexico	103714963	A6
Lugo, Maximano	27-Sep-1951	8-Jun-1898	Mexico	103714964	A223
Lugo, Pete	24-Jun-1924	1889	Mexico	103714965	161
Luna, Angel Quijada	5-Jul-1955	22-Oct-1882	Bisbee, AZ	103714966	A264
Lundberg, Ben Edgar	25-Mar-1948	9-Nov-1894	Oregon	103714967	A144
Lunde, Thomas A.	6-Feb-1962	8-Oct-1885	Montana	103714968	A392
Lundgren, Ben	5-Feb-1921	1-Oct-1880	Sweden	103714969	unk
Lung, Wong	24-Feb-1921		China	103714970	unk
Lushen, George	30-May-1921	12-Mar-1861	Austria	103714972	unk
Luthringer, John	11-Mar-1937	28-Dec-1901	Ohio	103714973	713
Lyly, Jack	14-Sep-1950	20-Jun-1887	Finland	103714974	A206
Lynch, Pat	16-Aug-1925	16-Mar-1860	Wisconsin	103714975	227
Lynn, James Ellis	4-Mar-1950	22-Feb-1886	Iowa	103714976	A199
Lyons, Annette	8-Jan-1925	4-Apr-1899	Louisiana	103714977	189
MacGillivray, Angus	9-Jan-1942	10-Apr-1901	Portland, Maine	103714978	891
Macias, Ygnacio Larez	1-Sep-1947	2-Feb-1895	Mexico	103714979	A123
Mack, Rosie	16-Jan-1951	1890	California	103714980	A214

52

Name	Death Date	Birth Date	Birth Location	FAG	Grave
Mackey, Nick Mick	1-Mar-1934	22-Dec-1884	Finland	103714981	594
MacNeil, Edwin	20-Oct-1937	9-Oct-1889	Ohio	65811588	737
Maeda, Carlos	5-Oct-1947	4-Nov-1909	Mexico	103714982	A127
Magdaleno, Jose	16-Jun-1961	3-May-1888	Mexico	103714983	A376
Magner, John	12-Nov-1935	17-Mar-1876	Texas	103714984	668
Magre, Edward	8-Jan-1939	17-Mar-1887	Italy	103714985	785
Maguire, Thomas	28-Feb-1924	11-Jun-1866	California	103714986	142
Mahoney, James	28-Nov-1933	4-Jul-1870	Illinois	103714987	587
Mahoney, John	5-Sep-1936	8-Nov-1890	Ireland	103714988	689
Maiden, Leeanna	2-Nov-1948	9-Oct-1921	Louisana	103714989	A166
Majnarec, Steve	25-Aug-1947	21-Dec-1892	Yugoslavia	103714990	A121
Make, Emil	14-Feb-1931	3-Jun-1890	Finland	103714991	459
Make, Oscar	11-Feb-1943	5-Jun-1883	Finland	103714992	931
Maki, Kalle	29-Mar-1934	16-Apr-1874	Finland	103714993	600
Maksimowich, Joseph	7-Jan-1943	15-Mar-1882	Poland	103714994	927
Malinarich, Anton	26-Sep-1926	10-Jun-1888	Austria	103714995	272
Mallet, Albert	3-Jun-1950	21-Jul-1875	Maine	103714996	A202
Mallory, Jack Vernon	25-Nov-1951	25-Feb-1902	California	103714997	A224
Maloney, Edward	18-Jan-1960	21-Mar-1908	Illinois	103714998	A351
Mangini, Dave	15-Dec-1942	9-Jul-1882	Rochester, NY	103714999	926
Manhiemer, Joe	12-Sep-1941	1-Jun-1922	Arizona	103715000	882
Manhire, Enos	9-Apr-1960	18-Apr-1886	England	102322241	A355

Robin Yonash

Name	Birth Date	Death Date	Birth Location	FAG	Grave
Mani, Jack	4-Feb-1897	12-Oct-1925	Switzerland	103715001	232
Mani, Joe	25-Aug-1887	21-Jul-1931	Spain	103715002	487
Mantez, Jose Marie	13-Feb-1876	19-Oct-1923	Mexico	103715003	128
Manzo, Tom	24-Dec-1877	17-Aug-1931	California	103715004	489
Marabel, Pete	30-Sep-1886	31-Jul-1929	Spain	103715005	391
Maraviles, Jim	6-Mar-1879	30-May-1923	Greece	103715006	114
Marcel, Manuel	12-Aug-1902	26-Jun-1971	Portugal	103715007	A474
Marcevich, Pete	5-Mar-1883	18-Jan-1923	Austria	103715008	unk
Marcheschi, Ernest	21-Jun-1894	8-Feb-1941	Italy	103715009	866
Mariano, Nick M.	1-Nov-1891	26-Nov-1941	Greece	103715010	888
Mariano, Tabios	14-Mar-1902	26-Apr-1926	Philippines	103715011	251
Mark, Margaret	26-Feb-1915	20-Jul-1933	California	103715012	571
Marks, Yung	19-Jun-1863	5-Apr-1941	China	99562154	868
Marquits, Stanley	4-May-1884	9-Jan-1944	Michigan	103715013	979
Martignoni, Ambrose	7-Dec-1879	9-Mar-1934	Italy	103715014	596
Martin, Byron F.	11-Mar-1910	15-Nov-1949	Colorado	103715015	A192
Martin, Doris	19-Sep-1903	7-Apr-1932	Utah	103715016	516
Martin, Frank	12-May-1878	15-Feb-1921	New York	103715017	unk
Martin, Griffin	30-May-1907	30-Jun-1967	Arkansas	102322567	A452
Martin, Hudson K.	10-Jun-1882	21-Dec-1938	El Dorado, CA	103715018	784
Martin, John	23-May-1894	3-Dec-1946	Massachusetts	103715019	A83
Martin, Joseph Frank	3-Mar-1875	6-Apr-1924	Italy	103715020	147

54

History of the Weimar Joint Sanatorium and the Weimar Cemetery

Name	Death Date	Birth Date	Birth Location	FAG	Grave
Martin, William P.	29-Oct-1948	19-Nov-1892	Missouri	103715021	A165
Martinac, Joe	6-Sep-1943	19-Mar-1887	Austria	103715022	963
Martinez, Adelberta	25-May-1928	22-Apr-1898	Mexico	103715023	342
Martinez, Francisco	25-Aug-1926	4-Oct-1894	Mexico	103715024	267
Martinez, Frank	10-Feb-1940	3-Mar-1918	Mexico	103715026	821
Martinez, Frank	1-Apr-1943	1-Nov-1892	Mexico	103715025	939
Martinez, Guadlupe	14-May-1932	6-Jan-1887	Mexico	103715027	521
Martinez, Joe	27-Mar-1929	20-Mar-1858	Mexico	103715028	382
Martinez, Joe	8-Sep-1921	29-Feb-1862	Spain	103715029	unk
Martinez, Jose	18-Feb-1944	19-Mar-1897	Mexico	103715030	985
Martinez, Manuel	26-Nov-1922	18-Apr-1888	Spain	103715031	unk
Martinez, Mary	13-Oct-1940	9-Jul-1926	Richmond, CA	103715032	849
Martinez, Romero	20-Jan-1957	2-May-1910	Arizona	103715033	A300
Martinez, Victor	1-Feb-1931	20-Feb-1883	Spain	103715034	456
Mascarini, John	18-Jun-1933	17-Nov-1914	Nevada	103715035	562
Mason, Tom	14-Jun-1921		California	103715036	unk
Masonich, Tom	9-May-1938	4-Oct-1885	Yugoslavia	103715037	763
Massey, Raymond	**21-Aug-1953**	**5-Sep-1898**	**Illinois**	**97521523**	**A243**
Matson, Charles	14-Nov-1931	6-Mar-1872	Finland	103715038	501
Matson, Peter W.	16-Feb-1946	16-Nov-1876	Sweden	103715039	A58
Matthews, Jesse Mack Green	3-Dec-1944	5-Oct-1878	Athens, AL	103715040	A16
Maulla, Luciano	30-Jan-1920	7-Jun-1877	Mexico	103715041	unk

55

Name	Death Date	Birth Date	Birth Location	FAG	Grave
Maxwell, Joseph	**19-Jan-1956**	**24-Oct-1885**	**Orange, NJ**	**97481417**	**A277**
Maynard, Willie	22-Nov-1966	18-Jan-1902	Texas	103715042	A446
Mays, Rudolph	17-Nov-1927	8-May-1906	Connecticut	103715043	315
McAuliffe, Dennis	1-Dec-1932	6-Jul-1882	Ireland	103715044	538
McCall, Eugene	11-Jun-1923	25-Sep-1857	Michigan	103715045	115
McCarty, Jack	29-Oct-1961	19-Apr-1880	Bellefonte, PA	103715046	A384
McCaul, Dudley	15-Nov-1946	22-Nov-1880	Virginia	103715047	A81
McClain, Flordia Ceola	30-Apr-1947	4-Sep-1927	Arkansas	103715048	A102
McCoy, Ralph	14-Dec-1945	3-Apr-1885	Oil City, PA	102280301	A55
McCullough, Isaac	17-Sep-1938	30-Sep-1882	Michigan	103715049	773
McDougall, Archie	30-Oct-1937	5-Oct-1856	Canada	103715050	738
McEachern, Archie	27-Jul-1943	12-Mar-1874	Toronto, Canada	103715051	959
McGee, John	2-May-1944	4-Aug-1875	Ireland	103715052	996
McGillivary, Dan	15-Mar-1927	9-Jun-1876	Nova Scotia	103715053	285
McGinity, Owen	10-Nov-1923	10-Mar-1858	New York	103715054	132
McGowan, Thomas	23-Oct-1924	23-Jan-1860	Pennsylvania	103715055	172
McGraw, George	13-Dec-1930	21-Jul-1881	Iowa	103715056	448
McGregor, Henry	30-Nov-1925	8-Oct-1905	Minnesota	103715057	241
McGuire, Arthur	9-Nov-1948	12-Dec-1880	California	38713610	A167
McHale, George	8-Jan-1944	1-Aug-1877	Buffalo, NY	103715058	978
McKay, Oscar	13-Jun-1946	15-Oct-1881	California	103715059	A72
McKinney, Dave	3-Mar-1948	11-Jun-1884	Illinois	103715060	A141

History of the Weimar Joint Sanatorium and the Weimar Cemetery

Name	Death Date	Birth Date	Birth Location	FAG	Grave
McKinnon, William	5-Mar-1940	23-Aug-1876	Calumet, MI	103715061	824
McLaughlin, Andrew	24-Sep-1922	29-Sep-1858	Connecticut	103715062	unk
McLaughlin, William	31-Dec-1924	9-Jul-1872	New York	103715063	188
McLeod, Allen	26-Dec-1939	15-Oct-1898	Ashland, WI	103715064	819
McMurtrey, Jesse	24-May-1958	12-Nov-1898	Hamburg, Iowa	103715065	A327
McNabb, Henry	7-Jan-1921	7-Jun-1882	Illinois	103715066	unk
McNeil, Edward H.	5-Jul-1949	21-Jun-1905	California	102316564	A184
McNulty, Richard	23-Mar-1926	13-Jun-1876	England	103715067	247
McRae, John	23-Jan-1947	2-Jul-1894	Canada	103715068	A87
McWhorter, Ruby	23-Apr-1940	1-Dec-1907	Los Angeles, CA	102230187	827
Meda, Pablo	24-Jun-1945	28-Jun-1896	Mexico	103715070	A38
Medina, Leonardo	22-Aug-1943	6-Nov-1882	Mexico	103715071	961
Medonda, Simon	10-Jun-1941	1-Jan-1871	Angels Camp, CA	103715072	875
Megallon, Jancito	14-May-1946	5-Jul-1912	Philippines	103715073	A70
Mejia, Luis	17-Feb-1938	21-Jun-1876	Mexico	103715074	756
Mejia, Profirio	22-Apr-1933	26-Feb-1920	Texas	99270318	557
Melendez, Manuel	4-Apr-1947	17-Jun-1889	Mexico	103715075	A99
Melshe, Wilhelm	12-Oct-1960	28-Mar-1872	Germany	103715076	A364
Meltzian, Gus	30-Aug-1934	5-Jan-1894	Germany	103715077	616
Mena, Alice Terrizon	25-Sep-1926	Sep-1902	Mexico	103715078	271
Mender, John R.	16-Oct-1924	29-Sep-1893	Italy	60064958	170
Meneffe, Rosalyn	22-Jan-1931	30-May-1913	California	103715079	453

57

Robin Yonash

Name	Birth Date	Death Date	Birth Location	FAG	Grave
Mera, Costa	5-Oct-1893	19-Mar-1927	Spain	103715080	286
Mesker, Charles	17-Apr-1858	23-Oct-1927	Canada	103715081	312
Meyers, David	20-Jul-1878	26-Aug-1927	Switzerland	103715082	303
Miajlovich, Sam	29-Nov-1884	25-Jun-1923	Serbia	103715083	119
Michler, Elmer H.	25-Jan-1906	30-May-1944	Fond du Lac, WI	102355191	A1
Middleton, Elizabeth	21-Jul-1879	22-Jul-1923	Maryland	103715084	122
Mileos, Gust	13-May-1890	25-Nov-1928	Greece	103715085	367
Miles, John J.	16-Mar-1874	30-Jan-1935	New York	103715086	636
Millare, Loy	29-Sep-1895	20-Sep-1924	Philippines	103715087	168
Miller, Alton E.	31-Jan-1909	21-May-1937	California	103715088	720
Miller, George	21-Jun-1874	19-Nov-1932	Michigan	103715089	536
Miller, Henry William	30-Oct-1892	30-Oct-1945	Port Townsend, WA	103715090	A50
Miller, Pete		26-Jun-1933	Montenegro	103715091	565
Minor, Wilbur A.	21-Jun-1898	25-Jul-1936	Tennessee	103715092	686
Miramontes, Tom		11-Mar-1939	Mexico	103715093	791
Miranda, muimSalome		31-Jul-1921		103715367	unk
Misanes, Alfredo	13-Jun-1908	15-Mar-1937	Philippines	103715094	714
Mitchell, Charles	15-Dec-1876	19-Jan-1932	Pennsylvania	103715095	511
Mitchell, Irving	19-Jun-1902	8-Mar-1935	California	103715096	643
Mitchell, Patrick	10-Feb-1868	7-Feb-1928	Iowa	103715097	329
Mitchell, Paul	25-Apr-1892	21-Dec-1961	Spain	103715098	A390
Mitchell, Raliegh	8-Dec-1894	23-Jan-1925	Georgia	103715099	191

58

History of the Weimar Joint Sanatorium and the Weimar Cemetery

Name	Death Date	Birth Date	Birth Location	FAG	Grave
Moe, Olaf	3-Oct-1940	27-Sep-1881	Norway	103715100	846
Moir, Hetherington	4-Jun-1965	18-May-1894	Canada	102193951	A428
Moki, Henry	27-Feb-1935	16-Sep-1889	Finland	103715101	641
Molina, Cruz	29-May-1938	Jun-1866	Mexico	103715102	764
Molina, Manuel	2-Sep-1941	25-Dec-1908	Florence, AZ	103715103	881
Molina, Sabes	31-Jan-1924		Mexico	103715104	139
Molinari, Andrew	19-Jun-1926	9-Apr-1869	Italy	103715105	260
Monarrez, Abraham	16-Apr-1935	16-Mar-1907	Mexico	103715106	647
Montes, Ysaias	22-May-1928	6-Jun-1900	Mexico	103715107	341
Moore, Fred E.	16-Jan-1947	24-Sep-1902	Missouri	103048390	A86
Moore, James	13-Oct-1922	13-Jan-1870	Oregon	103715108	unk
Moraila, Joseph	29-Sep-1966	22-Oct-1905	Mexico	103715109	A441
Moralez, Cruz	25-May-1964	14-Sep-1904	New Mexico	103715110	A417
Moran, John	29-Nov-1966	17-Jul-1897	New Jersey	103715111	A447
Moreland, John	6-Jul-1922	26-Oct-1863	Wisconsin	103715112	unk
Moreno, Ruth	13-Dec-1936	4-May-1915	Kansas	103715113	706
Morgan, Arthur	4-Nov-1937	4-Jul-1881	Canada	103715114	740
Morkovich, Sam	26-Oct-1934	26-Jan-1885	Serbia	103715115	626
Morrell, Albert	21-Apr-1948	13-Jun-1881	Canada	103715116	A147
Morris, Bertha	30-Jul-1947	27-Jul-1907	Virginia	103715117	A114
Morris, Eula Mae	28-Nov-1946	24-Apr-1913	Oklahoma	103715118	A82
Morris, Hardy	30-Oct-1953	16-Jun-1886	Nesbitt, MS	103715119	A246

59

Robin Yonash

Name	Birth Date	Death Date	Birth Location	FAG	Grave
Morris, James	16-Aug-1862	29-Jan-1931	Maine	103715120	455
Morrison, Margaret	22-May-1907	19-May-1965	Wyoming	103715121	A425
Morrison, Murray	2-Jan-1885	11-Oct-1937	Massachusetts	103715122	736
Morrissey, Edmund	2-Feb-1863	4-Mar-1932	Illinois	103715123	514
Morrow, Thomas F.	5-Apr-1892	26-Mar-1934	Austria	103715124	599
Mosguda, Besente		26-Sep-1921	Mexico	103715125	unk
Moss, Fred	16-Apr-1864	28-Jan-1925	Utah	103715126	192
Moyes, Joseph	20-Mar-1896	22-Jun-1940	Ogden, Utah	102230811	841
Mugan, James	18-Apr-1882	30-Jun-1930	California	103715127	424
Muimauno, Dominico0	24-Sep-1893	1-Apr-1922	Italy	103715128	unk
Mullarkey, Mike	1879	17-Nov-1924	Ireland	103715129	176
Mullen, John	10-Jun-1864	24-Oct-1925	Ireland	103715130	235
Mulvaney, Tom	20-Oct-1864	18-Sep-1933	Ohio	103715131	578
Mummert, Edward	18-May-1901	23-Jan-1943	Milwaukee, WI	103715132	928
Munsee, John	11-Apr-1894	24-Jun-1956	Montana	103715133	A291
Murakis, Joseph	1886	5-Jan-1924	Greece	103715134	136
Murley, James A.	9-Mar-1863	18-Jul-1927	California	103715135	296
Murovich, Matt	24-Oct-1884	13-Jun-1943	Yugoslavia	103715136	949
Murphy, Bert	4-May-1897	21-Nov-1960	Boston, MA	103715137	A366
Murphy, Raymond Joseph	5-Jun-1897	30-Aug-1949	Maryland	102316651	A190
Murphy, Robert	31-Mar-1892	30-Jan-1963	California	103715138	A400
Murray, Henry	5-Aug-1872	20-Jul-1933	New York	103715139	570

Name	Death Date	Birth Date	Birth Location	FAG	Grave
Murray, John	5-Aug-1922	27-Aug-1898	New York	103715140	unk
Murray, Ozra Ellis	30-Sep-1948	6-Apr-1870	Maine	103715141	A161
Murrieta, Miguel G.	21-Aug-1949	24-Nov-1900	Mexico	103715142	A189
Musser, Vernon	25-Oct-1928	12-Jan-1903	Japan	103715143	364
Myers, Emery A.	3-Mar-1956	16-Oct-1907	Wisconsin	103715144	A282
Myllyla, Karle	2-Feb-1960	17-Nov-1885	Finland	103715145	A353
Nadal, Helen	1-Jul-1928	12-Feb-1909	Philippines	103715146	345
Nagata, K.	20-Mar-1920	23-Apr-1879	Japan	103715147	unk
Nalpin, William	5-Jan-1922	11-Apr-1885	Pennsylvania	103715148	unk
Negrete, Ramon H.	24-Sep-1956	31-Aug-1888	Mexico	103715149	A295
Nelson, Anton	20-Dec-1961	23-Feb-1881	Norway	97470822	A389
Nelson, Antone	**17-May-1921**	**31-Jul-1863**	**Norway**	**103715150**	**unk**
Nelson, Carl E.	10-Jan-1941	7-Feb-1881	Kansas City, MO	103715151	864
Nelson, Edward	26-Apr-1946	22-Apr-1890	Norway	103715152	A65
Nelson, Martin	20-Mar-1925	1-Apr-1884	Minnesota	103715153	201
Nelson, Nels	31-Oct-1944	7-Dec-1870	Sweden	103715154	A15
Nelson, Nelse Axel	23-Jul-1924	25-Jun-1877	Finland	103715155	163
Nelson, Oscar	24-Aug-1922	17-Jan-1886	Sweden	103715156	unk
Nevarez, Frank Chavera	23-Aug-1947	12-May-1911	Texas	103715157	A120
Newhouse, Spivey	30-May-1947	14-Feb-1923	Texas	103715158	A107
Nichols, John	23-Apr-1956	28-Oct-1885	Missouri	103715159	A287
Nides, Roberto	20-Mar-1946	15-Jan-1900	Mexico	103715160	A62

61

Robin Yonash

Name	Death Date	Birth Date	Birth Location	FAG	Grave
Nieto, Felicitas	29-Apr-1939	18-May-1913	Mexico	103715161	796
Niles, Walter	20-Jan-1928	16-Mar-1869	Wisconsin	103715162	326
Nir, Charles	15-Dec-1922	3-Feb-1877	Austria	103715163	unk
Nixon, Henry G.	30-Mar-1942	7-Jul-1875	Yreka, CA	103715164	900
Noe, Orville	12-Oct-1966	4-May-1905	Illinois	103715165	A444
Nolan, John E.	8-Jan-1953	23-Mar-1883	California	103715166	A239
Noll, Adolph	11-May-1946	2-Mar-1878	California	103715167	A68
Nona, G. Andrew	19-Jul-1920	28-Aug-1878	Italy	103715168	unk
Norden, John	30-Jul-1942	12-Feb-1869	England	103047195	905
Norman, Lee	**18-Dec-1965**	**3-Jul-1902**	**Missouri**	**97580563**	**A433**
Northcott, George	3-Nov-1938	1-Oct-1889	San Francisco, CA	103715169	777
Norton, George	**12-Dec-1942**	**24-Aug-1899**	**Waterbury, CT**	**103715170**	**923**
Nush, Michael	16-Jun-1925	8-Apr-1905	Pennsylvania	103715171	214
Nyholm, Carl	25-May-1933	26-Dec-1877	Finland	103715172	561
Oakes, Mary	17-Nov-1926	18-Sep-1900	Kentucky	103715173	274
Obera, Tomasa	2-Oct-1929	25-Aug-1889	Mexico	103715174	402
Oblizalo, Nick	5-Feb-1931	6-Dec-1882	Dalmatia	103715175	458
O'Brien, James	19-Apr-1947	14-Feb-1891	San Francisco, CA	103715176	A101
O'Brien, Patrick	18-Apr-1930	26-Feb-1876	California	103715177	419
O'Bryan, John	5-Oct-1927	15-Aug-1857	Wisconsin	103715178	306
Occioni, Peter	10-Mar-1937	20-Jun-1886	Italy	103715179	712
O'Connor, Ennis	2-Mar-1928	24-Aug-1898	Ireland	103715180	332

62

Name	Death Date	Birth Date	Birth Location	FAG	Grave
Odon, Ferdinand	11-Jun-1923	30-Jul-1875	Russia	103715181	116
O'Grady, Maurice E.	14-Oct-1920	4-Oct-1878	Boston, MA	103715182	unk
Ogrin, Jim	25-Aug-1939	26-Jul-1890	Austria	99273160	809
Oja, Atle	27-Feb-1956	21-Jul-1883	Finland	103715183	A280
Olsen, Gus	12-Oct-1920	14-May-1878	Sweden	103715184	unk
Olsen, Hilda	10-Sep-1929	3-Nov-1887	Wisconsin	103715185	399
Olson, Gust	28-Jan-1938	1882	Sweden	103715186	751
Olson, John	26-Sep-1943	6-Jun-1891	Sweden	103715187	965
O'Neal, Patrick	30-May-1941	6-Jun-1882	Georgetown, CO	103715188	872
O'Neil, Jack	**16-Mar-1942**	**17-Mar-1876**	**Hopland, CA**	**97517469**	**897**
O'Neil, Samuel Jack	12-Mar-1951	12-Jan-1913	Texas	103715189	A217
O'Neil, Tom	26-Feb-1930	9-Jan-1878	Missouri	103715190	414
O'Neil, William R.	12-Aug-1933	30-Oct-1867	Minnesota	103715191	573
Opeka, John	10-Feb-1928	17-May-1887	Hawaii	103715192	330
Ordonez, Quirina	9-Feb-1940	4-Jul-1910	Mexico	103715193	820
Ortez, Isobel	18-Sep-1927	19-Nov-1911	Mexico	103715194	304
Osborne, Mary	3-Nov-1940	20-Jul-1914	Fostoria, Ohio	103715195	852
Oscoff, George	5-Aug-1925	5-Aug-1905	Kansas	103715197	224
Owen, William W.	3-Jan-1921	9-Jun-1868	Ohio	103715198	unk
Owens, James	19-Sep-1947	12-Mar-1891	Mississippi	103715199	A125
Owens, Joseph	22-Sep-1952	3-Nov-1883	Des Moines, Iowa	103715200	A233
Padilla, Juanita	26-Mar-1934	19-Dec-1918	Mexico	103715201	598

Robin Yonash

Name	Death Date	Birth Date	Birth Location	FAG	Grave
Pagan, Angel	16-Jun-1923	1-May-1901	Hawaii	103715202	117
Pagoa, Thomas	3-Jun-1935	Feb-1908	Philippines	103715203	653
Palmeri, Pete	11-Aug-1949	25-Dec-1888	Italy	103715204	A188
Palmquist, John	16-Apr-1944	10-Apr-1879	Sweden	103715205	992
Pappas, Chris	15-Aug-1933	1885	Greece	103715206	574
Pappas, Chris	8-Jun-1941	1874	Greece	103715207	874
Pappas, Nick	30-Apr-1968	6-Apr-1885	Greece	103715208	A461
Pardini, Mansueto	25-Aug-1964	25-Mar-1882	Italy	103715209	A419
Parizek, Carl	4-Mar-1934	15-Dec-1879	Germany	103715210	595
Parks, Walter	14-Apr-1949	16-Jun-1887	Arkansas	103715211	A180
Partin, James	12-Dec-1939	18-Oct-1874	Mendocino Co., CA	103715212	818
Pasini, Jasper	12-Jan-1921	25-Dec-1869	Italy	103715213	unk
Pasiona, Aurie	5-Aug-1921	21-Jan-1889	Philippines	103715214	unk
Pastorini, Andrew	27-Sep-1934	18-Jun-1887	Italy	103715215	621
Patterson, Pat	3-Jun-1934	17-Nov-1875	Illinois	103715216	606
Patton, Jesse	25-Dec-1944	2-Jun-1889	Nashville, TN	103715217	A20
Patton, Matilda	7-Mar-1970	13-Mar-1900	Wyoming	103715218	A468
Pavich, Joe	23-Sep-1936	18-Mar-1893	Austria	103715219	692
Penaflor, Alex Cruz	1-Jun-1950	3-May-1902	Mexico	103715220	A203
Pender, Ollie	23-Dec-1952	11-Sep-1882	Texas	103715221	A238
Pennell, Willard	15-Dec-1942	16-Jan-1881	Wilmington, DE	103715222	925
Penuniri, Manuel	28-Oct-1946	17-Jun-1898	Mexico	103715223	A80

History of the Weimar Joint Sanatorium and the Weimar Cemetery

Name	Death Date	Birth Date	Birth Location	FAG	Grave
Perani, Gabriel	25-Apr-1932	6-Jan-1879	Italy	103715224	518
Perez, Brigido M.	24-Apr-1950	16-Feb-1903	Mexico	103715225	A200
Perez, Feliciano	24-Mar-1957	14-May-1898	Mexico	103715226	A307
Perez, Jose Leon	15-Mar-1945	3-Mar-1917	Mexico	103715227	A29
Perez, Justo	18-Jun-1937	13-Feb-1885	Spain	103715228	722
Perez, Loujina	15-Dec-1930	1901	New Mexico	103715230	450
Perez, Lupe	1-Jul-1931	12-Dec-1911	Mexico	103715231	484
Perez, Profirio—see Mejia, Profirio					
Perez, Severiano P.	26-Sep-1928	21-Feb-1889	Mexico	99269240	362
Perez, Victor	25-Mar-1937	13-Jun-1910	Mexico	103715232	715
Perry, Louis	**1-Mar-1955**		New Mexico	**97531248**	**A262**
Pertico, Joe	22-May-1929	1891	New Mexico	103715233	385
Peters, Martin	6-Oct-1927	25-Feb-1899	California	103715234	309
Petersen, Chris	12-Feb-1938	11-Oct-1869	Denmark	103715235	755
Peterson, Gus	22-Jan-1922	12-Oct-1872	Wisconsin	103715236	unk
Peterson, Gust	12-Oct-1943	11-Nov-1885	Sweden	103715237	968
Peterson, Joe	19-Jul-1925	3-Oct-1871	Sweden	103715238	219
Peterson, Peter	28-Oct-1930	9-Jan-1885	Denmark	103715239	446
Petranovich, Joseph	27-Nov-1959	9-Mar-1887	Yugoslavia	103715240	A349
Petrini, Pietro	21-Feb-1925	10-Aug-1880	Italy	103715241	197
Petroski, Frank	10-Oct-1942	22-Jul-1892	Poland	103715242	914
Petty, Jack O.	30-Mar-1931	7-Nov-1878	Illinois	103715243	465

65

Robin Yonash

Name	Death Date	Birth Date	Birth Location	FAG	Grave
Peyton, Frank M.	8-Jun-1931	18-Jun-1890	Ohio	103715244	479
Pike, Frank	5-May-1931			103715245	473
Pilovich, George	2-Feb-1939	16-Jun-1896	Yugoslavia	103715246	787
Pimentel, Esequiel	9-Feb-1963	3-Apr-1894	Mexico	103715247	A402
Pine, Antone	21-Sep-1940	10-Apr-1908	Point Richmond, CA	103715248	845
Pineda, Louis	14-Dec-1931	3-Oct-1896	Philippines	103715249	504
Pinon, Alfredo	19-Aug-1928	3-Jun-1902	Mexico	103715250	356
Pioletti, Bart	12-Dec-1928	5-May-1883	Italy	103715251	368
Placido, Freido	30-Mar-1931	4-Oct-1904	Philippines	103715252	464
Plasensia, Domingo	6-Jan-1929	12-May-1888	Mexico	103715253	373
Plouff, George	12-Jun-1948	26-Aug-1874	Wisconsin	102316172	A151
Polacio, Ignacio	22-Jul-1934	31-Jul-1885	Mexico	103715254	612
Polideri, Alfred	4-Oct-1932	1886	Italy	103715255	530
Polino, Sabino	7-Oct-1931	30-Dec-1901	Mexico	103715256	497
Ponce, Francisco	16-Jan-1946	4-Oct-1905	Mexico	103715257	A56
Popovich, Peter	21-Aug-1923	15-Jul-1882	Austria	103715258	125
Portillo, Ramon	11-Aug-1937	7-Sep-1898	Mexico	103715259	732
Potter, June L.	4-May-1925	23-Feb-1875	Kentucky	103715260	208
Powers, Arthur	10-Aug-1947	26-Jun-1884	Massachusetts	103715262	A117
Powers, Nicholas	12-Jun-1931	19-Aug-1861	Michigan	103715263	481
Pozanovich, Mike	9-Jun-1935	13-Jul-1889	Yugoslavia	103715264	655
Prager, Harry	21-May-1933	14-Apr-1887	South Dakota	103715265	559

Name	Death Date	Birth Date	Birth Location	FAG	Grave
Preston, Fred	5-May-1926	1-Jan-1868		103715266	252
Previsich, John	11-Feb-1925	15-Aug-1894	Slavonia	103715267	196
Prieto, Nicholas	5-Feb-1961	10-Sep-1890	Mexico	103715268	A368
Prijatel, Charles	2-Jul-1933	8-Jan-1900	Minnesota	99562314	567
Prommel, Joe	9-Jun-1945	16-Jan-1887	Paterson, NJ	103715269	A37
Pudas, Eino	2-Oct-1946	12-Jan-1899	Sweden	103715271	A79
Pullo, Vincent	28-Sep-1930	15-Apr-1910	Philippines	103715272	441
Pumar, Modesto	1-Aug-1927	15-Mar-1878	Spain	103715273	297
Purtell, Walter	6-Jan-1947	17-Jun-1900	Massachusetts	102280688	A85
Quayle, John J.	31-Aug-1928	21-Jun-1872	Michigan	103715274	359
Quinn, A. M.	15-May-1922	7-Jun-1872	Alaska	103715275	unk
Quintoro, Teodoro	4-Feb-1945	19-Sep-1887	Mexico	103715276	A26
Quy, Slim	31-Jan-1933	1891	Albania	103715277	548
Raboy, Joe	27-Jan-1925	6-Feb-1895	Philippines	103715278	193
Racich, William	13-Aug-1942	17-Sep-1921	San Pedro, CA	94672198	910
Raineri, Jene	26-Aug-1921	19-Jul-1898	California	103715279	unk
Ralya, Nick	12-Nov-1920	15-Oct-1854	Austria	103715280	unk
Ramaila, Pastro	7-Feb-1935	5-May-1912	Hawaii	103715281	637
Ramaila, Rose	29-Apr-1932	16-Sep-1918	Hawaii	103715283	519
Ramirez, Bajilio	10-Jun-1931	Jan-1900	Mexico	103715284	480
Ramirez, Lorenzo	28-Nov-1959	10-Aug-1888	Mexico	103715285	A350
Ramirez, Pilar	21-Jan-1928	23-Oct-1887	Mexico	103715286	325

Robin Yonash

Name	Death Date	Birth Date	Birth Location	FAG	Grave
Ramirez, Rufino Ressa	9-Aug-1943	10-Jul-1884	Mexico	103715287	960
Ramirez, Thomas	8-Feb-1947	29-Dec-1919	Mexico	103715288	A92
Ramos, Angel	16-May-1945	Jun-1890	Philippines	103715289	A34
Ramos, Cristobal	16-Nov-1928	1903	Spain	103715290	365
Ramos, Frank	17-Dec-1926	3-Jul-1898	Colorado	103715291	279
Ramos, Miguel	18-Jun-1923	3-Aug-1883	Mexico	103715292	118
Ramos, Paul	28-Apr-1946	5-Jan-1920	Philippines	103715293	A67
Ramsdale, Chester	**10-May-1951**	**7-Nov-1897**	**Wisconsin**	**9746919**	**A219**
Randall, William Oran	22-Nov-1948	11-Oct-1870	Wisconsin	103715294	A169
Rangel, Virginia	10-Apr-1939	25-Apr-1908	Las Cruces, NM	103715295	795
Raper, George	20-Nov-1941	21-Feb-1898	Winfield, KS	102235126	887
Rapesora, Pedro	28-Nov-1935	15-Jun-1916	Philippines	103715296	671
Ratkovich, John	6-Feb-1945	4-Apr-1885	Yugoslavia	103715297	A25
Ratliff, O. T.	19-Aug-1947	8-Aug-1913	Arkansas	103715298	A119
Ratto, Pietro	2-Mar-1947	2-Aug-1871	Italy	103715298	A96
Ratuita, Sixto	22-Dec-1937	1-Aug-1910	Philippines	103715300	743
Raymond, George	12-Oct-1932	7-Jul-1876	Alaska	103715301	531
Red, Aughty	21-Jun-1933	23-Apr-1903	Oklahoma	103715302	563
Reed, Edgar	10-Mar-1948	28-Aug-1899	Washington	103715303	A142
Reid, Thomas	16-Mar-1933	26-Sep-1877	New York	103715304	554
Reinheller, Gustav	16-Aug-1958	26-Dec-1899	North Dakota	103715305	A331
Relacion, Tom	16-Sep-1933	24-Jan-1898	Philippines	103715306	577

68

History of the Weimar Joint Sanatorium and the Weimar Cemetery

Name	Death Date	Birth Date	Birth Location	FAG	Grave
Rember, Arthur	20-Jan-1954	28-Mar-1897	Hailey, Idaho	103051748	A249
Renteria, Peter	10-Apr-1927	2-Jun-1901	Mexico	103715307	288
Reval, Antoine	16-May-1926	16-Nov-1876	France	103715308	254
Reyes, Luciano	15-Jun-1943	7-Jan-1900	Mexico	103715309	950
Rice, Chester Francis	12-May-1943	8-Aug-1877	San Francisco, CA	103715310	946
Rice, George	24-Jan-1932	29-Sep-1882	West Virginia	103715311	512
Richards, Arthur	24-Apr-1935	15-Apr-1881	Michigan	103715312	648
Richards, Marion	24-Dec-1929	11-Nov-1890	Iowa	103715313	407
Ricketts, Richard Allen	16-Nov-1940	16-Oct-1886	Bieber, CA	43447279	854
Rico, Julio	18-Jan-1938	12-Apr-1907	Mexico	103715314	748
Rigdon, Clarence	27-Dec-1940	20-Jan-1914	Greenville, SC	103715315	862
Riley, Harry	18-Oct-1924	31-Aug-1880	Illinois	8696473	173
Riley, Hugh J.	14-Nov-1932	17-Jun-1887	New York	103715316	535
Rios, Jose	10-Nov-1945	19-Mar-1882	Mexico	103715317	A53
Ritchie, John	22-Dec-1924	16-Apr-1874	New Hampshire	103715318	186
Riutta, Waino	30-Nov-1954	2-Sep-1903	Michigan	103715319	A258
Riyu, Tamijiro	6-Feb-1958	24-Mar-1881	Japan	103715320	A323
Roberts, George	7-Jan-1934	2-Apr-1894	Austria	103715321	591
Roberts, Harry	19-Nov-1956	24-Jan-1889	Illinois	103715322	A297
Roberts, John C.	17-Mar-1923	8-Mar-1874	Maine	103715323	unk
Robey, Floyd	28-Sep-1963	Oct-1885	Virginia	103715324	A410
Robinson, Bill	4-Mar-1963	23-Mar-1895	Oklahoma	103715325	A403

Robin Yonash

Name	Death Date	Birth Date	Birth Location	FAG	Grave
Roca, Gian	5-Oct-1935	16-Aug-1897	Switzerland	103715326	664
Rocha, Frank	14-May-1947	Oct-1905	Mexico	103715327	A104
Rodden, Charles	6-Jun-1931	11-Feb-1866	Ireland	103715328	477
Rodrigues, Elsie Fay	22-Feb-1947	10-Jan-1929	California	102281303	A95
Rodrigues, Francisco	31-Aug-1968	9-Oct-1886	Portugal	103715329	A464
Rodrigues, Joe	22-Jun-1930	24-Aug-1884	Spain	103715330	422
Rodriguez, Mariano	9-May-1940	24-Jan-1886	Spain	103715331	832
Rodriquez, Avelino	30-May-1965	10-Jun-1890	El Paso, TX	103715332	A426
Rodriquez, Eucarnacion	20-Oct-1935	14-Apr-1873	Mexico	103715333	666
Rodriquez, Marciana	24-Aug-1927	6-Nov-1902	Mexico	103715334	301
Roeder, William	13-Nov-1924	23-Jan-1903	Germany	103715335	175
Roemmich, Margaret	2-Aug-1962	10-Mar-1920	Ireland	103715336	A396
Roff, Gus	25-Jan-1933	1-Jun-1900	Russia	103715337	549
Rogers, Hugh	1-Jan-1932	26-Jun-1885	Ireland	103715338	510
Ronald, James	22-Dec-1921	27-Oct-1876	Canada	103715339	unk
Rosalez, Trinidad	13-Feb-1936	Mar-1920	Mexico	103715341	679
Rosas, Tiburcio	28-Feb-1957	11-Aug-1901	Mexico	103715343	A303
Roswell, Joseph Albert Jr.	31-Aug-1940	31-Aug-1940	Weimar, CA	103715344	844
Roth, August	24-Aug-1957	8-Feb-1887	Russia	103715346	A314
Rotha, Thomas	31-May-1921	Oct-1842	Texas	103715347	unk
Rowe, Fred	16-Apr-1926	11-Apr-1880	England	103715348	248
Rowe, William Charles	31-Aug-1943	14-Dec-1874	Iowa	103715349	962

History of the Weimar Joint Sanatorium and the Weimar Cemetery

Name	Death Date	Birth Date	Birth Location	FAG	Grave
Roy, Demetris	14-Mar-1928	1902	Philippines	103715350	334
Rozewski, Felix	5-Apr-1934	14-May-1890	Poland	103715351	601
Rubek, Mike	16-Apr-1925	24-Apr-1899	Austria	103715352	205
Rubio, Jose	16-Nov-1961	19-Mar-1900	Mexico	103715353	A387
Ruhstaller, Louis	12-Jun-1934	3-Aug-1905	Switzerland	103715354	607
Ruiz, Julian	9-Nov-1936	9-Apr-1888	Mexico	103715355	699
Ruiz, Ramon	15-May-1948	4-Oct-1906	Mexico	103715356	A148
Ruiz, Ramon	12-Aug-1965	31-Aug-1908	Mexico	103715357	A431
Saari, Charles	25-Sep-1948	10-Jun-1891	Finland	103715358	A159
Sabedra, Ramon	4-Dec-1924	13-Sep-1897	Spain	103715359	181
Sacchi, Remos	19-Jul-1941	10-Jun-1903	Italy	103715360	880
Sagazzi, Andrea	24-Mar-1924	13-Mar-1871	Italy	103715361	146
Salas, Pedro	20-Apr-1923	1877	Colorado	103715362	110
Salate, George/Joe	26-Aug-1927	28-Feb-1880	Italy	103715363	302
Sale, John	13-Feb-1937	20-May-1888	Italy	103715364	710
Sales, Milliard	12-Feb-1925	15-Mar-1888	Kansas	103715365	195
Salmen, Frederick Elis	3-Oct-1950	3-Dec-1896	Finland	103715366	A207
Salo, Gus	28-Sep-1939	25-Jun-1882	Finland	101798033	810
Salque, Peter	20-Jun-1965	25-Feb-1903	California	103715368	A429
Salvador, Severino	28-Jan-1949	11-Feb-1901	Philippines	103715369	A173
Sanchez, Jesus	5-Aug-1942	15-Apr-1937	Woodland, CA	103715370	909
Sanchez, Miguel	21-Apr-1950	22-Dec-1904	Texas	103715371	A201

Robin Yonash

Name	Death Date	Birth Date	Birth Location	FAG	Grave
Sanchez, Pedro	23-Dec-1940	1892	Mexico	103715372	860
Sanchez, Rafael	6-Nov-1925	21-Jan-1895	Mexico	103715373	239
Sandberg, Morris	8-Apr-1956	28-Mar-1885	Stratford, Iowa	103715374	A285
Sandford, Harry	27-Oct-1924	5-Mar-1891	Australia	103715375	174
Sandoval, Abigail	12-Oct-1934	15-Aug-1918	Arizona	103715376	624
Sandoval, Guillermo	25-Oct-1958	10-Feb-1903	Mexico	103715377	A335
Sandoval, Ignacia	25-Sep-1934	~1891	Mexico	102194621	619
Sandoval, Joe	14-Apr-1930	15-Mar-1903	Mexico	103715378	418
Santana, Jose	26-May-1947	18-Jul-1905	Mexico	103715379	A106
Santellano, Margaret	4-Dec-1936	20-Jul-1899	Mexico	103715380	703
Santiago, Luciano	6-Jul-1928	12-Jan-1896	Philippines	103715381	346
Santillanes, Gregoria	15-Jul-1946	9-Jun-1922	New Mexico	103715382	A73
Santos, Salvador	25-Jul-1932	~1891	Spain	103715383	523
Sanwick, Clarence L.	**6-Feb-1952**	**8-Nov-1894**	**Minnesota**	**97518615**	**A229**
Sarge, John	21-Aug-1930	25-Jan-1883	Poland	103715384	432
Sarich, Tony	11-Dec-1923	22-Jun-1895	Austria	103715385	134
Savage, James	18-Mar-1942	5-May-1886	San Francisco, CA	103715386	898
Scanlon, Michael	27-Apr-1923	24-Nov-1882	Ireland	103715387	112
Schaaf, William	5-Jul-1926	16-Aug-1876	California	103715388	261
Schanuel, Edward	19-Aug-1942	9-Dec-1883	Denver, CO	102249454	912
Schmick, Aleck	27-Jan-1938	25-Nov-1893	Russia	103715389	750
Scholer, Ethelyn	15-Nov-1954	26-Oct-1904	Texas	103715390	A257

72

Name	Death Date	Birth Date	Birth Location	FAG	Grave
Schooley, Roy	14-Mar-1957	28-Aug-1901	Texas	103715391	A306
Schrader, Walter	29-May-1945	1-Sep-1878	Utica, NY	103715392	A35
Schuell, William	5-Mar-1930	10-Mar-1865	California	103715393	415
Schuster, James	23-Jun-1965	14-Oct-1884	Wisconsin	103715394	A430
Schwedencoff, Dan	11-Feb-1921	Oct-1875	Russia	103715395	unk
Scott, David	24-Oct-1939	18-Feb-1917	Palmer, TN	94672345	811
Sears, Louise	19-Mar-1940	27-Apr-1906	Italy	8642660	825
Seavey, Harry	3-Jan-1948	16-Aug-1884	Iowa	8642664	A133
Sedlacek, John	7-Sep-1930	29-May-1875	Nebraska	103715397	438
Service Hugh F.	5-Aug-1942	15-Nov-1890	Scotland	103715398	908
Setogawa, Sumitaro	5-Oct-1947	9-Feb-1876	Japan	103715399	A128
Seton, Allen	24-Mar-1943	20-Mar-1896	Scotland	103715400	937
Sevr, Thomas	18-Mar-1938	Dec-1886	Austria	103715401	759
Shaft, John	24-Aug-1966	2-Feb-1882	New York	99285764	A440
Shaughnessy, William	23-Nov-1942	Dec-1879	Ireland	94672570	919
Shaver, Harry	14-Sep-1920	15-Jan-1883	North Dakota	103715402	unk
Shaw, Billy	21-Oct-1952	23-Dec-1926	Nevada	103715403	A235
Shebley, Homer S.	17-Sep-1937	3-Mar-1906	California	103715404	734
Sheffield, Charles E.	30-Sep-1934	10-Mar-1875	Nova Scotia	103715405	622
Sherer, Claude	23-Jul-1942	10-Apr-1892	Sencea, MO	102236719	904
Sherry, Frank	11-Mar-1922	8-Apr-1857	New Jersey	103715406	unk
Shewmake, Raymond	6-Jan-1957	24-Jan-1918	Kansas	103715407	A299

73

Robin Yonash

Name	Death Date	Birth Date	Birth Location	FAG	Grave
Shinn, Dallwon W.	16-May-1943	18-Feb-1873	Korea	103715408	947
Shintani, T.	5-Apr-1933	1885	Japan	103715409	556
Shively, Delbert F.	27-Jul-1950	9-May-1874	New York	102195926	A204
Shock, Don	23-Nov-1926	4-Nov-1865	Pennsylvania	103715410	278
Sholtz, John	19-Jul-1962	14-Sep-1888	Pennsylvania	103715411	A395
Shubert, Arthur Max	26-Jan-1938	20-Jan-1869	Germany	103715412	749
Silva, Dolores	17-Nov-1930	14-Jul-1884	Mexico	103715413	447
Silva, Frank	24-Jul-1945	19-Jul-1891	San Francisco, CA	103715414	A42
Silva, Theresa	29-Nov-1939	2-Nov-1922	Milpitas, CA	103715415	817
Silveria, Joseph	3-May-1934	22-Nov-1885	Azores	103715416	605
Simmons, Joseph	31-Jul-1925	2-Mar-1886	England	103715416	221
Simmons, Milton	25-Sep-1936	1-Dec-1886	Texas	103715418	693
Simms, Charles	17-Jul-1936	6-Aug-1882	Colorado	103715419	650
Singh, Catherine	21-Jul-1939	14-Feb-1937	Madera, CA	103715420	806
Siordia, Raul	30-Aug-1926	7-Dec-1904	Mexico	103715421	268
Skalski, Albert	9-Apr-1942	13-Apr-1893	Buffalo, NY	103715422	901
Skelly, Dan York	7-Dec-1967	20-Jul-1899	Texas	102322711	A460
Skoog, Fred	9-Apr-1935	7-Aug-1884	Finland	103715423	646
Slater, Oscar	24-Jan-1952	25-Jun-1888	California	103715424	A227
Slinger, Alice Mary	16-Jun-1943	17-Jul-1917	Minneapolis, MN	102250643	952
Smiley, Alfred	20-Aug-1921	12-Jan-1868	Mexico	103715425	unk
Smith, Audrey	18-Jan-1965	31-Mar-1930	Louisiana	103715426	A423

74

History of the Weimar Joint Sanatorium and the Weimar Cemetery

Name	Death Date	Birth Date	Birth Location	FAG	Grave
Smith, Frank	5-Jan-1938	1890	Illinois	103715427	746
Smith, Frank Benton	27-Aug-1931	1-Aug-1899	Oklahoma	103715428	493
Smith, Howard	4-May-1956	~1910	Missouri	103715429	A289
Smith, Joseph J.	4-Apr-1928	12-Sep-1883	New York	103715430	336
Smith, LeRoi	17-Jul-1968	9-Feb-1902	Clinton, Iowa	103715431	A462
Smith, Lester	24-Apr-1958	22-Dec-1890	Lodi, MS	102319882	A325
Smith, Lowell	24-May-1940	27-Nov-1885	White Haven, PA	103715432	834
Smith, Richard	15-Nov-1942	22-Apr-1877	Jamestown, CA	103715433	917
Smith, Walter	13-Oct-1946	29-Sep-1886	Pennsylvania	103715434	A78
Smoljo, Ely	26-Feb-1940	1-Jul-1896	Austria	103715435	823
Snyder, John	18-Dec-1931	17-Jun-1886	Minnesota	103715436	505
Solis, Porfirio	5-Jun-1961	15-Apr-1883	Mexico	103715437	A375
Soliz, Gabriel	14-Mar-1944	18-Mar-1889	Mexico	103715438	988
Solon, George	9-Apr-1923	25-Apr-1887	Greece	103715439	108
Solores, Bincelado	9-Aug-1929	5-Feb-1885	Mexico	103715440	396
Solorio, Saturnino	15-Aug-1944	1915	Mexico	103715441	A8
Sonders, Charles L.	27-May-1935	21-Oct-1901	Missouri	103715442	651
Sorensen, Soren	6-Nov-1961	2-Sep-1902	Denmark	103715443	A386
Soria, Besenta	10-Apr-1930	5-Apr-1905	Mexico	103715444	417
Soto, Jose	1-Oct-1968	20-Nov-1890	Mexico	103715445	A465
Soto, Louis	19-Dec-1952	Aug-1907	Mexico	103715446	A237
Soto, Reynaldo	9-Mar-1929	3-Aug-1894	Mexico	103715447	380

Name	Death Date	Birth Date	Birth Location	FAG	Grave
Soule, Thomas	10-Oct-1934	22-Jun-1866	Maine	103715448	623
Spalding, Arthur	2-Nov-1937	20-Apr-1888	San Francisco, CA	103715449	739
Spencer, William	**2-Jun-1960**	**23-Sep-1911**	**Webb City, MO**	**97451878**	**A360**
Spinden, Chris	7-Nov-1920	27-Aug-1860	Switzerland	103715450	unk
Sproul, Frank	30-Mar-1963	2-Apr-1884	unknown	103715451	A405
St. Arnault, Robert E.	**15-Jan-1958**	**9-Sep-1924**	**Fall River, MA**	**97531536**	**A322**
St. Gregory, Samuel	2-Jan-1963	24-Apr-1899	Spain	103715452	A398
Stack, Jack	12-Oct-1922	16-Oct-1878	Illinois	103715453	unk
Stamer, Nellie	28-Dec-1947	9-Aug-1906	Illinois	103049744	A132
Stanley, Peter	22-Jun-1936	15-Dec-1875	Illinois	103715454	685
Starr, Frank	16-May-1947	26-May-1901	Kentucky	103715455	A105
Stats, Adolph	13-Sep-1942	8-Nov-1872	Junction City, KS	103715456	17
Staver, Edna Pauline	9-Jul-1947	17-Apr-1910	Missouri	102281523	A111
Steele, Ralph	24-Aug-1924	5-Jul-1884	Connecticut	103715457	164
Steen, Charles	4-Jan-1920	20-Mar-1866	Sweden	103715458	unk
Steilen, George	31-May-1938	21-Apr-1907	Evanston, IL	103715459	766
Steinwandt, Jacob	5-Nov-1960	25-Oct-1906	Bismarck, ND	103715460	A365
Stenhund, Magnus	28-Jan-1928	12-Feb-1900	Finland	103715461	328
Stephens, Walter H.	24-Jun-1951	16-Oct-1882	Oregon	103715462	A221
Stevens, Albert N.	15-Dec-1935	26-Jul-1890	Missouri	103715463	674
Stevenson, Justin	18-May-1965	3-Feb-1892	California	103715464	A424
Stewart, Charles	3-Apr-1935	26-Jun-1888	Massachusetts	103715465	645

History of the Weimar Joint Sanatorium and the Weimar Cemetery

Name	Death Date	Birth Date	Birth Location	FAG	Grave
Stewart, Elizabeth Alfatza	6-Feb-1948	23-Oct-1907	California	103715466	A136
Stewart, James	13-Sep-1952	12-Nov-1887	Indiana	103715468	A232
Stewart, John	13-Feb-1926	8-Dec-1874	New York	103715469	244
Stewart, Stephen	8-Dec-1932	24-Jan-1869	New York	103715470	543
Stewart, Willis	4-Jul-1939	7-May-1895	Belton, TX	102229981	802
Stier, Albert	27-Jul-1947	25-Jan-1910	Ohio	103715471	A113
Stinson, Ralph L.	23-Jun-1930	2-Jan-1874	Ohio	103715472	423
Stockman, Ben	11-Jun-1940	13-Dec-1873	Sweden	103715473	839
Street, Cecil	26-Apr-1943	16-Feb-1898	Princeton, MO	103715474	942
Strickland, Edward	11-Feb-1936	26-May-1905	California	103715475	677
Strickland, Laurence	18-Aug-1932	3-Mar-1866	Louisiana	103715476	526
Stringer, Harry	20-Jul-1943	~1883	Vallejo, CA	103040457	957
Strobel, George	18-Aug-1925	6-Feb-1851	Germany	103715477	228
Stromberg, Charles E.	29-Jul-1950	15-May-1888	Wisconsin	103715478	A205
Strype, William	13-Apr-1961	3-Jan-1892	Holland	103715479	A373
Stuart, Donald	15-Sep-1928	14-Feb-1860	Canada	103715480	361
Stucker, Louis	14-Jan-1937	15-Mar-1863	Switzerland	103715481	708
Sturm, Robert	6-Sep-1944	29-Jul-1877	Germany	103715482	A10
Suan, T.	15-Jun-1924		Philippines	103715483	158
Suarez, Joe	15-Jan-1930	Nov-1889	Spain	103715484	409
Suarez, Ramon	26-Nov-1967	28-Aug-1905	Arizona	103715485	A459
Sudbay, Otis	12-Oct-1958	7-Jul-1889	Gloucester, MA	103715486	A334

Robin Yonash

Name	Death Date	Birth Date	Birth Location	FAG	Grave
Sullivan, John	17-Mar-1922	10-Mar-1880	Canada	103715487	unk
Sullivan, John Francis	16-Dec-1954	1-Nov-1909	Massachusetts	103715488	A259
Sullivan, Tim	30-Jul-1920	6-Jan-1869	Connecticut	103715489	unk
Sumpter, Barney	16-Jul-1937	16-Apr-1904	Arkansas	103715490	724
Sundberg, Arthur	4-May-1937	4-Dec-1884	Sweden	103715491	719
Sundquist, Gustaf Arthur	25-Sep-1943	1-Apr-1900	Finland	103715492	964
Sutton, Merle	6-Jun-1956	13-Dec-1905	Oklahoma	103265558	A290
Swanson, Leonard	28-Mar-1925	9-Apr-1883	Sweden	103715493	202
Swick, Dick	20-Apr-1945	11-Dec-1892	Austria	98172674	A34
Symenysh, Fred	1-Aug-1942	15-Feb-1897	Russia	103715494	907
Takanen, Ivar	28-May-1938	20-Aug-1882	Greenland	103715495	765
Takemoto, Matsutaro	9-Dec-1948	18-Mar-1880	Japan	103715496	A170
Taktar, Jack	28-Feb-1937	15-May-1885	Finland	103715497	711
Tamm, John	4-Feb-1927	27-Feb-1879	Russia	103715498	281
Tanaka, Sansaku	20-Apr-1949	25-Sep-1879	Japan	103715499	A181
Tanaya, Josephine	13-Aug-1938		Sacramento, CA	103715500	772
Tarpie, Louis	2-Nov-1931	17-Mar-1888	California	103715501	500
Tartini, T.	31-May-1925	1900	Sacramento, CA	103715502	210
Taylor, Warner	16-Apr-1928	7-Nov-1900	Virginia	103715503	337
Taylor, William Louis	25-Mar-1970	10-Jan-1897	Maine	103715504	A469
Tena, Diego	13-Jul-1925	1881	Spain	103715505	218
Tenetti, Pete	2-Aug-1945	11-Nov-1884	Italy	103715506	A44

History of the Weimar Joint Sanatorium and the Weimar Cemetery

Name	Death Date	Birth Date	Birth Location	FAG	Grave
Terry, Silas	8-Jun-1948	29-Apr-1894	Missouri	102315987	A150
Thompson, Edward	24-Nov-1955	25-Jun-1885	Sweden	103715507	A272
Thompson, Frank	26-May-1958	Nov-1891	Brooklyn, NY	103715508	A328
Thompson, Jack	17-Jun-1955	19-Jul-1902	Washington	103715509	A263
Thompson, James Owens	10-Aug-1935	1-Aug-1903	Iowa	103715510	658
Thompson, Newman	26-Jan-1922	21-Jul-1888	Mississippi	103715511	unk
Thompson, Rosa	23-Nov-1938	28-Nov-1898	Wisconsin	99272864	782
Thompson, Severt	17-Jan-1945	5-Mar-1884	Wisconsin	103715512	A23
Thompson, Tom	10-Feb-1942	22-May-1910	Norway	103715513	895
Thornton, Daniel	13-Jan-1926	1886	New York	103715514	243
Thornton, Frank	7-Aug-1925	6-Dec-1899	California	103715515	223
Tillotson, Charles	6-Oct-1940	30-Jun-1877	Suisun, CA	103040067	848
Toland, James	31-Oct-1961		Canada	103715516	A385
Tolipolos, Nick	12-Mar-1926	8-Jun-1882	Greece	103715517	246
Tomasi, Eugenio	19-Aug-1955	4-Jan-1895	Italy	103715518	A266
Tona, Evaristo	19-Sep-1932	1898	Mexico	103715519	528
Toriotis, George	27-Dec-1924	14-Feb-1888	Greece	103715520	187
Tornberg, John	22-Apr-1931	1891	Sweden	103715521	472
Torres, Frank	5-Mar-1957	29-Jan-1902	New Mexico	103715522	A305
Torres, Louis	3-Dec-1955	15-Aug-1885	Mexico	103715523	A273
Torres, Steve	17-Sep-1941	18-Nov-1898	Garfield, NM	103715524	884
Tracia, Aleck	9-Feb-1961	25-Dec-1905	New York	103715525	A369

79

Robin Yonash

Name	Birth Date	Death Date	Birth Location	FAG	Grave
Tracy, Jack	22-May-1887	18-Apr-1946	California	103715526	A64
Tracy, John	1-Mar-1874	23-Dec-1933	England	103715527	589
Trasvira, Ysabel	1891	8-Jul-1931	Mexico	103715528	485
Travers, Joseph	13-Jul-1906	30-Oct-1957	Manchester, MA	102318976	A319
Travinsky, John	24-Dec-1891	7-Mar-1947	Russia	103715529	A97
Trimaisch, Francis	6-Jan-1889	17-Apr-1922	Austria	103715530	unk
Tsagranis, Nick	7-Mar-1888	27-Sep-1957	Greece	103715531	A317
Turk, Daisy M.	14-May-1919	23-May-1952	Alabama	103715532	A231
Turner, Frank	12-Jun-1888	26-Apr-1944	Boston, MA	103715533	995
Tuzich, John	22-May-1881	12-Jan-1933	Russia	99561910	547
Tyler, Geraldine	9-Jun-1921	20-Jan-1956	Oregon	103715534	A278
Unkovich, Chris	22-May-1895	29-Dec-1922	Austria	103715535	unk
Upham, Arthur	14-Feb-1882	25-Feb-1949	Ohio	102316472	A176
Upton, Harry	5-Dec-1876	14-Feb-1936	Tennessee	103715536	680
Uranga, Aneceto	27-Jun-1897	10-Aug-1966	Texas	103715537	A439
Urenda, Juan	24-Jun-1882	16-Feb-1961	Mexico	103715538	A370
Urich, Bob	28-Oct-1888	14-Apr-1942	Yugoslavia	103715539	902
Uzelac, Sam	24-Mar-1886	15-Apr-1941	Yugoslavia	103715540	869
Valdez, Francisco	4-Oct-1897	31-Aug-1961	Mexico	103715541	A381
Valdez, Pedro	1-Aug-1905	5-Mar-1929	Mexico	103715542	377
Vales, James	7-Mar-1884	26-Dec-1925	Greece	103715543	242
Vallecillo, Esteban	28-Nov-1906	3-Sep-1928	Mexico	103715544	360

History of the Weimar Joint Sanatorium and the Weimar Cemetery

Name	Death Date	Birth Date	Birth Location	FAG	Grave
Valverde, Genevieve	8-Feb-1947	2-Jan-1895	Texas	103715545	A94
Van Dalfsen, Jochem	2-Sep-1956	27-Oct-1875	Holland	103715546	A296
Van Horn, James	19-Dec-1931	15-Jan-1871	Missouri	103715547	507
VanAlmen, Frank William	10-Oct-1947	26-May-1882	Minnesota	103715548	A129
Vandiver, Thomas	3-Aug-1961	5-Sep-1892	Alaska	103715549	A379
Vargas, Fred	30-Jan-1960	14-Feb-1912	New Mexico	103715550	A352
Vargas, Jose	19-May-1960	1-Dec-1893	Mexico	103715551	A358
Vargas, Marcus	3-Feb-1952	1-Jan-1885	Portugal	103715552	A228
Vasquez, Juana	28-Nov-1935	24-Jun-1897	Mexico	103715553	670
Vasquez, Victor	12-Jun-1927	Jan-1887	Mexico	103715554	293
Veci, Augustine	30-Sep-1941	1897	Spain	103715555	886
Vega, Ramon	14-Mar-1951		Arizona	103715556	A216
Vega, Teodora	8-Jun-1929	24-Apr-1871	Mexico	103715557	387
Velasco, Frank	1-Oct-1933	23-Sep-1909	Hawaii	103715558	580
Vereskoski, Carlo	13-Jul-1923	26-May-1882	Russia	103715559	121
Verlin, Steve	4-Oct-1940	16-Jun-1885	Austria	103715560	847
Veselich, John	5-Feb-1964		Austria	103715561	A413
Vesterfelt, William	31-Jan-1959	6-Apr-1887	New York	102320142	A341
Vidas, Jack	14-Apr-1925	24-Jul-1886	Austria	103715562	204
Viereck, Fred	11-Apr-1956	21-Jun-1885	Germany	103715563	A286
Villa, Jose	11-Jun-1937	31-May-1904	Mexico	103715564	721
Villa, Manuel	30-Nov-1934	24-Nov-1906	Mexico	103715565	629

81

Robin Yonash

Name	Death Date	Birth Date	Birth Location	FAG	Grave
Vincent, Leonard	30-Oct-1958	22-May-1910	England	94671586	A336
Vino, Aino	2-Sep-1930	4-Dec-1882	Finland	103715566	436
Vinson, Edgar	28-Feb-1945	15-May-1900	Houston, TX	103715567	A27
Viramontes, Nicholas	15-Apr-1931	10-Sep-1888	Mexico	103715568	470
Viskovich, Joseph	3-Jan-1936	19-Mar-1884	Austria	103715569	675
Vittorio, Alfonso	23-Oct-1924	7-Feb-1886	Spain	103715570	171
Vivarelli, Gus	31-Mar-1931	16-Apr-1880	Italy	103715571	466
Vogeli, Henry H.	19-Jul-1939	15-Feb-1894	Oneida, CA	98471756	-
Wagner, Frank	28-Feb-1959	18-Jun-1899	Hungary	103715572	A342
Walima, Hans	16-Sep-1941	3-Jan-1893	Finland	103715573	883
Walker, Charles William	8-Sep-1923	21-Oct-1876	Illinois	103715574	126
Walker, Orlando	22-Nov-1956	4-Jan-1900	Florida	103715575	A298
Wallace, Andrew	15-Jun-1966	8-Feb-1884	Denmark	103715576	A436
Wallace, Pat	17-May-1921	Dec-1879	Ireland	103715577	unk
Walls, Lucius	29-Sep-1948	15-Jan-1923	Louisiana	103715578	A160
Walsh, Harry	26-Oct-1935	17-Apr-1882	Ireland	103715579	667
Walsh, James	14-Oct-1931	6-Feb-1880	Ireland	103715580	499
Ward, Thomas	1-Nov-1939	4-Sep-1882	New York, NY	103715581	813
Ward, William Clay	25-Aug-1926	22-Feb-1865	Ireland	103715582	266
Warner, John	4-Mar-1943	3-Mar-1880	Gunnison, CO	103715583	934
Warren, Matthew	10-Nov-1950	28-Jan-1897	Finland	103715584	A210
Wearne, Leo E.	4-Feb-1927	29-May-1878	Michigan	103715585	282

82

Name	Death Date	Birth Date	Birth Location	FAG	Grave
Webb, Albert	17-Feb-1943	16-May-1869	Texas	103715586	933
Webber, William G.	8-Oct-1944	15-Jun-1884	Toledo, Ohio	103715587	A12
Weber, William	23-Aug-1927	30-Jun-1870	Germany	103715588	300
Webster, Thomas W.	9-Jun-1927	25-Mar-1870	California	103715589	291
Weckstrom, Axel	13-Jul-1925	29-Dec-1869	Sweden	103715590	216
Weddel, Arthur Wesley	4-Jul-1943	21-Aug-1913	Dunsmuir, CA	94671916	953
Weigand, Peter	1-Dec-1942	22-Feb-1880	Russia	103715591	920
Welch, John D.	15-Apr-1934	17-Nov-1874	Ohio	103715592	602
Welch, Robert	20-Mar-1942	2-Jul-1880	Menominee, WI	103715593	899
West, Olaf	12-May-1946	29-Dec-1878	Sweden	103715594	A69
Westman, Santra	22-May-1922	29-Apr-1881	Finland	103715595	unk
Wheeler, Guy	27-Dec-1940	26-Aug-1884	Shreveport, LA	103715596	861
White, Enoch Milton	28-Apr-1943	7-Mar-1874	Salinas, CA	102250158	944
Whitman, Frank	30-Mar-1930	11-Jul-1888	California	103715597	416
Wilcockson, Thomas C.	21-Aug-1961	12-May-1910	Arkansas	103715598	A380
Wilkinson, Leroy	30-Jan-1933	15-Aug-1882	Kansas	103715599	550
Williams, Charles	18-Jul-1929	25-Jul-1881	Virginia	103715600	389
Williams, George F.	29-Apr-1935	13-Jan-1874	West Virginia	4744155	649
Williams, Joan	9-Jan-1964	8-Jul-1932	Massachusetts	103715601	A412
Williams, William Edgar	11-May-1924	15-Sep-1876	Washington	103715602	154
Willsey, Edward	10-Mar-1934	26-Oct-1905	Washington, DC	103715603	597
Wilson, Arthur	17-Sep-1944	1-Jun-1874	Finland	103715604	A11

Robin Yonash

Name	Death Date	Birth Date	Birth Location	FAG	Grave
Wilson, Frank	4-Mar-1921	1882	Ohio	103715605	unk
Wilson, George V.	28-Mar-1921	2-Feb-1873	Oregon	103715606	unk
Wilson, John L.	17-Nov-1920	28-Apr-1860		103715607	unk
Wilson, Ralph	27-Mar-1923	4-Feb-1886	Missouri	103715608	unk
Wilson, Tom	6-Jun-1938	1-Jun-1871	Illinois	103715609	767
Wilson, William	22-Apr-1923	22-Nov-1886	Louisiana	103715610	111
Wimbari, John	21-Dec-1931	17-Feb-1884	Finland	103715611	506
Wimmel, James Orville	18-Sep-1936	8-Aug-1906	Missouri	98172560	690
Wing, Ah	27-Feb-1941	27-Jul-1851	China	103715612	867
Witt, Harry	24-May-1933	29-May-1874	Pennsylvania	103715613	560
Wolf, William	5-Jan-1928	31-Aug-1885	Illinois	103715614	322
Wong, Ah	4-Nov-1920	1862	China	103715615	unk
Wong, Back Shing	17-Sep-1957	1-Jan-1887	China	103715616	A316
Wong, Chung Way	12-Jun-1944	24-Aug-1908	China	103715617	A3
Wong, Emma	22-Apr-1928	14-Jun-1902	California	103715618	339
Wong, Warren	20-May-1935	21-Jun-1922	California	98172331	650
Woodcock, Howard	2-Oct-1933	11-Aug-1887	Maryland	103715618	581
Woody, Hezekiah	19-Jun-1972	25-Nov-1900	South Carolina	103715621	A475
Woulas, Chris	4-Apr-1931	24-May-1878	Greece	103715622	468
Wozniak, Mieczyslau Francis	6-Mar-1954	12-Aug-1900	Illinois	103715623	A250
Wyss, Ernest	2-Aug-1945	16-Jun-1885	Switzerland	103715624	A45
Yamaguchi, K.	5-Feb-1920	1877	Japan	103715625	unk

84

History of the Weimar Joint Sanatorium and the Weimar Cemetery

Name	Death Date	Birth Date	Birth Location	FAG	Grave
Yarbrough, James	27-Oct-1968	20-Nov-1880	Washington	102323149	A466
Yazaki, Hirosaki	19-Jul-1927	11-Nov-1857	Japan	103715626	295
Yee, Harry Bean	**1-Apr-1949**	**2-Jul-1893**	**California**	**103715627**	**A179**
Yepez, Jose	18-May-1944	19-Mar-1906	Mexico	103715628	999
Yerkovich, George	13-May-1961	6-May-1890	Yugoslavia	103715629	A374
Young, Arthur Charles	15-Nov-1962	2-Sep-1888	South Dakota	103715630	A397
Young, Ernest	11-Jan-1930	29-Apr-1906	Washington	103715631	408
Young, Mildred	9-Oct-1930	1-Jan-1908	California	103715632	443
Young, William	31-Jan-1942	10-Oct-1873	Lexington, MO	103715633	894
Zacharias, Anthony G.	25-Nov-1928	12-Jan-1890	Greece	103715634	366
Zambetti, Fidal	23-Apr-1924	29-Feb-1876	Italy	103715635	150
Zamora, Conception	7-Oct-1927	8-Dec-1882	Mexico	103715636	308
Zizgakos, John	15-Jan-1922	16-Jun-1868	Greece	103715637	unk
Zuzich, John—see Tuzich, John (death certificate has both names)					

ABOUT THE AUTHOR

Robin Yonash grew up in rural Iowa Hill, California in the 1950's and then went off to college and business. Following a successful career in the computer field, she retired in 1998 and moved back to her beloved Sierra Nevada foothills where she has engaged in various volunteer projects. In 2012 she started The Weimar Project, a joint effort which included members of the community, the Colfax Area Historical Society, the Colfax Veterans of Foreign Wars California Post 2003, and the American Legion Colfax Post 192 District #7, all located in Colfax, Placer County, California, to honor the people, including veterans, buried in the Weimar Cemetery.

www.ingramcontent.com/pod-product-compliance
Lightning Source LLC
Chambersburg PA
CBHW071057290526
45795CB00004B/1544